Praise for
Be The Difference Now

The CEO's Blueprint for Cultures That Perform and Leadership That Lasts

"*Be the Difference Now* marks a watershed moment in the evolution of conscious leadership.

Woven with the wisdom of The BoardRoom—a collective of past leadership legends—this book disrupts the status quo of hierarchical leadership and calls each of us to awaken and lead from a paradigm of wisdom, presence, alignment, and connection. In an era shaped by rapid technological change and increasing depersonalization, it is an essential guide for those committed to leading at the edge of what's possible."

Safire Rose
Author of *Awakening, Awakening* and *Rose Petals*
Ventura, California
www.safire-rose.com

"*Be The Difference Now* is a refreshing antidote to the conformity that too often dilutes leadership. This book shows how authenticity and empathy aren't just nice-to-haves—they're the very qualities that create lasting impact.

I trust every page because the principles here aren't theory; they're lived experience. Donna has walked this path herself, and it shows. A must-read for anyone ready to lead with courage, presence, and heart."

John Shea
Corporate Communications
Amtrak
Washington, D.C

"Donna DiDomenico has a unique way of addressing modern leadership with clarity and empathy. *Be The Difference Now* will inspire and empower you to lead with presence, purpose, and authenticity."

Susan Hornberger
HR & Project Management Professional
Robbinsville, New Jersey

"Finally, a book that understands the pressures of the executive seat and offers a path to lead with clarity and courage. Thank you, Donna, for this empowering guide!"

Dr Barry Auchettl, Chief Visionary
Life Vision Academy
Ft. Lauderdale, Florida
www.lifevisionacademy.com

"In *Be The Difference Now*, Donna's voice—amplified by the wisdom of The BoardRoom—invites readers to deepen their understanding of what it truly means to lead. This book is a powerful guide for conscious leadership, offering transformative insights on how to build cultures rooted in change, community, connection, and unity.

I highly recommend this book to anyone in a leadership or managerial role who is ready to lead with clarity, presence, and purpose."

Susan B. Mercer, Spiritual Alchemist
Author of *A Graceful Goodbye: A New Outlook on Death*
Stevensville, MD
www.modernoutlooks.com

"*Be The Difference Now* is a powerful invitation to lead differently—from the inside out anchored in clarity, presence, and the courage to evolve. It bridges the human and the strategic, offering a path for leaders to move beyond performance and into lasting impact—not by doing more, but by leading from who they truly are."

Candace Lindner
CEO and Founder of *Summit People Strategies*
Long Valley, New Jersey
www.summitpeoplestrategies.com

"*Be The Difference Now* is more than a good read—it's a call to lead with presence, truth, and soul. The insights within are both timeless and urgently needed. Donna doesn't just write about leadership—she lives it. I've had the privilege of working alongside her and witnessing the power of her approach in action. This is how I know this book will change how you lead, how you show up, and how you see yourself."

Benjamin Sims
VP People and Culture
Austin Texas

"Donna DiDomenico has created more than a leadership book, she has created a movement. *Be The Difference Now* is a powerful blend of clarity, soul, and strategy for the executive ready to lead with purpose. It's the kind of book that doesn't just inform, it transforms."

Marilyn Alauria
Author and Creator of *Next Level Living*
Marin County, California
www.marilynalauria.com

"Far from your typical leadership book, *Be The Difference Now* inspires CEOs to embody what all of us look for in a leader and organization culture."

Paul Pavlica
Talent and Culture Champion
Chevy Chase, Maryland
www.linkedin.com/in/paul-pavlica/

"If you are an executive intending to craft a successful career leading high-performing teams and organizations, *Be the Difference Now* is mandatory reading and reference for your future. The old leadership paradigms are insufficient to carry our society into the future and Donna's LEADER Archetype is the roadmap that every executive must have to forge a new path forward for themselves and the organizations they lead."

Sarina Arcari, award winning transformation executive
Co-founder, *The O+Positive Way*
Washington DC Metro Area
www.opositiveway.com

"*Be the Difference Now* is a fresh, powerful take on leadership for today's world. Donna invites us to lead from presence and purpose—not just position. This book isn't just for CEOs, but for anyone who wants to create impact where they are.

With wisdom from The BoardRoom woven throughout, every chapter offers inspiration and practical guidance. It's insightful, energizing, and easy to read.

Grab your highlighter—*Be the Difference Now* will change how you lead, and how you live."

Sue Carol Shalley
Retired CEO, *Field Services Unlimited*
Huntington Beach, California
www.linkedin.com/in/sue-shalley-11791913

"*Be The Difference Now* is a "must read" that will excite experienced managers to re-awaken the truths they have always known and will shape their legacy."

Patricia Wilson
Sales Manager
Harbor Freight Tools
Howell, New Jersey

"Donna has captured the essence of what it takes to lead in a world that won't wait. Bold, insightful, and deeply human, *Be The Difference Now* activates the intuitive leader in all of us."

Veronica L. Nabizadeh, Esq.
Author of *Don't Throw in the Towel Yet!:If It's Worth Fighting About, It's Worth Fixing*
Jacksonville, Florida
www.MarriageRelationshipRestart.com

"There has never been a more crucial time for a book like *Be The Difference Now*. In an era where so many feel disconnected and discouraged, Donna offers a fresh model of leadership grounded in heart, courage, and presence. Her practical guidance and profound insights are not only easy to implement but also create a lasting ripple of impact—personally, professionally, and organizationally. This book is both timely and timeless, a call to lead differently and make a real difference now."

Susan Sisk
Money and Business Coach
Bismarck, North Dakota
https://www.linkedin.com/in/susan-sisk-85644939

BE THE DIFFERENCE NOW

BE THE DIFFERENCE NOW

THE CEO'S BLUEPRINT FOR CULTURES THAT PERFORM AND LEADERSHIP THAT LASTS

DONNA DIDOMENICO

Waterside Productions

Disclaimer: The information contained in this book is for educational and informational purposes only. The insights, stories, and strategies shared are based on the author's professional experience, personal observations, and interviews with organizational leaders. They are intended to inspire thoughtful reflection and support leadership development in a rapidly evolving business landscape.

This book does not constitute legal, financial, or psychological advice, nor does it guarantee specific outcomes for individuals or organizations. Readers are encouraged to apply discernment and consult with qualified professionals when making decisions related to business operations, leadership practices, or organizational culture.

Names and identifying details may have been changed to protect the privacy of individuals. Any resemblance to real persons, living or dead, is purely coincidental.

The author and publisher disclaim any liability for any loss or risk incurred as a direct or indirect consequence of the use and application of any of the contents of this book.

First Printing, 2025

ISBN-13: 978-1-968401-16-0 print edition
ISBN-13: 978-1-968401-17-7 ebook edition

Waterside Productions
2055 Oxford Ave
Cardiff, CA 92007
www.waterside.com

__This book is dedicated to:__

The leaders rising into a world not yet imagined.
You are the pulse of what comes next.

ACKNOWLEDGMENTS

I am deeply grateful to my husband, Anthony, for supporting me through every phase of this journey—loving me as I've grown and changed and letting go even when holding on tighter might have been easier. Your steady presence and quiet encouragement have meant everything.

To my precious daughter, Alyssa—your presence in my life has transformed the way I see the world. You've shown me, more than anyone, the profound impact a single leader can have. You are my daily reminder of why this work matters.

Heartfelt thanks to Dr. Susan L. Reid for your endless support, guidance, and mentorship throughout this process. Your patience and coaching helped me bring this book to life in a way that is both meaningful and impactful.

To Marilyn Alauria, thank you for inspiring my spiritual growth and supporting me as I expanded into new levels of awareness and clarity.

To Susan Hornberger and Candace Lindner, thank you for lending your sharp proofreading and editorial brilliance to this project. As you all know, proofreading is not my gift, and I'm so grateful it is yours. Your attention to detail ensured this work reflects its best self.

To my wonderful friends, thank you for walking alongside me with love, encouragement, and belief—reminding me to keep going even when the path felt never-ending.

To The BoardRoom, thank you for never failing me. You bring insight, clarity, and the energy of change as we navigate a rapidly shifting world and rebuild the structures that no longer serve.

Thank you to Gayle Gladstone, CEO of Waterside Productions, and her amazing team for your support and insights throughout this publishing journey.

Finally, to all my colleagues and collaborators—thank you for your creative minds and innovative spirits. You've enriched my work in ways I couldn't have done alone. Your contributions have made my work richer and more alive. Together, we're building what's next.

TABLE OF CONTENTS

FOREWORD

Chip Conley

I've been leading companies since I was 26.

Now in my 60s, I've had the privilege of witnessing—and helping shape—multiple eras of leadership. From founding *Joie de Vivre Hospitality*, the second-largest operator of boutique hotels in the U.S., to serving as Airbnb's Head of Global Hospitality and Strategy during its meteoric rise, and now as the founder of *Modern Elder Academy* (MEA), the world's first midlife wisdom school, I've learned this: leadership is a living, evolving thing. And right now, it's undergoing its most radical transformation yet.

That's why Donna's book, *Be The Difference Now*, couldn't be more timely—or more necessary.

Over the last 30 years, business and management schools have adopted the notion that effective leadership begins with active listening.

The 'servant leader' concept was a significant leap from command-and-control models. But Donna takes us even further. She doesn't just propose a shift—she demands it. She asserts, with unmistakable clarity and empathy, that the future can't afford to wait for leaders to evolve. We can't afford to take another decade—or even another year—to get it right. We need leaders who embody the shift now.

At the heart of Donna's framework is a deeply human premise, rooted in the French concept of *noblesse oblige*: with power comes responsibility—not just to perform, but to elevate others. In a world that's increasingly diverse, distributed, and demanding something more, *Be The Difference Now* offers a blueprint for leaders who are ready to meet the moment.

And let's talk about that moment.

By 2027, most people in the American workforce will report to a boss younger than they are, according to the U.S. Department of Labor Workforce Projections. The majority of college graduates today are women, and our leadership future will reflect that. Diversity—in gender, age, thought, ethnicity—isn't a political stance. It's a demographic reality. Donna speaks to this with nuance and foresight, using "Sam," her gender-fluid stand-in for CEO leadership, to reflect a future that's inclusive, dynamic, and real.

But perhaps what struck me most is Donna's courage to push against outdated narratives. In an era where anti-DEI sentiment is making headlines and some leaders are retreating to the outdated, John Wayne-esque bravado of "might makes right," she offers something profoundly different: the LEADER Archetype. This model proves that the most effective leaders of tomorrow will look nothing like the leaders of yesterday—and that's not a threat to excellence. It's the very source of it.

Donna's writing is not just insightful and passionate, it's also highly practical. She doesn't just offer theories—she offers wisdom earned on the ground. Her perspective is both refreshing and revolutionary, and her vision is one I deeply believe in. After reading her book, you'll feel inspired and equipped to lead in the future.

If you're a CEO, read this book. If you're an emerging leader, read this book. If you care about the future of work, the health of your teams, and the kind of legacy your leadership leaves behind—read this book.

The future of leadership is not only younger and more female—it's also more attuned, more inclusive, and more aware than ever. Donna has given us a powerful guide to rise and meet it. Her book makes it clear that everyone, regardless of gender, age, or background, has a crucial role to play in shaping this future.

—Chip Conley
NY Times bestselling author and founder of the *Modern Elder Academy*

Preface

If we lead as we always have, we will encounter
the same challenges and achieve the same result.
The future demands more. ~ The BoardRoom

The Origins of This Book

The room fell silent. Papers rustled. Chairs were pushed back.

People stood to leave—and I knew something was wrong.

The strategy we had outlined was sound. The objectives were clear.

But as I looked around the room, I didn't see the engagement or the belief that would carry it forward.

And that's when it hit me:

The future of the company was at stake.

The decisions we made—and the leadership we demonstrated—would change everything.

This wasn't just important; it was the difference between movement and stagnation, between evolution and decline.

Yet even with a strong strategy and clear direction, something critical was missing: real connection, shared ownership, and the energy that turns ideas into action.

And in that moment, I realized: Leadership isn't about how well you speak.

It's about what you ignite in others.

In leadership, it's not what you say that shapes the future—it's what you awaken.

This book was born from moments like that—and from decades spent navigating leadership environments where results were prioritized over relationships, and power often overshadowed purpose.

I began my career in the 1980s, when executive leadership was rarely questioned and often misused. Over time, the language evolved, and the strategies became more polished. Yet one thing remained: too many leaders still led from fear, ego, or habit. Too few led with clarity, compassion, and presence. I felt this deeply—not only in meetings but also in people's lives.

Leadership doesn't end at the office door; it echoes through homes, relationships, and communities. It shapes how people perceive themselves and their futures.

And I've always believed we can do better.

Because today, the stakes have changed. Leaders no longer just influence business results—they shape cultures, industries, and futures with every decision they make.

That belief is the essence of this book.

Leading from a Different Place

This book is about leadership that connects—leadership that brings out the best in others, not through force, but by example. It's about honoring the responsibility we hold—not just to hit our goals, but to elevate others.

I've led for most of my life—in classrooms, on teams, and in the boardroom. For decades, I've trained, mentored, coached, and advised executive leaders through mission-critical decisions and cultural transformation. I've always felt called to lead differently: to question what no longer serves, to ask better questions, to trust something deeper.

The Writing Journey

Writing this book gave me an opportunity to reflect—not only on what I've learned but also on what I've had to unlearn. It brought clarity to truths I had lived but never fully articulated. There were moments when the words flowed easily and others when I had to wrestle with my own growth, vulnerability, and resistance.

The writing process surprised me: the more I wrote, the more I healed.

With each page, I returned to the kind of leader I believe we're all capable of becoming.

In that stillness, something new emerged: Leadership is not about being perfect. It's about being present. It's about knowing who you are—and leading from that place, especially when others are watching, waiting, and following.

Sam's Top-Down Effect and Gender-Fluid Leadership

You'll meet Sam throughout this book as the embodiment of the Top-Down Effect—a living example of how one leader's inner alignment ripples across an entire organization. I intentionally chose Sam to be gender fluid because the future of leadership won't be confined by outdated binaries.

Leadership is evolving. It's no longer about leaning into polarized roles. It's about blending masculine with feminine, strategy with intuition, clarity with compassion, and strength with empathy.

Chip Conley, founder of the *Modern Elder Academy* speaks to this shift: tomorrow's leaders won't just mirror the demographics of today's workforce—they'll embody an energetic presence rooted in balance, emotional fluency, and inner clarity.

Sam reflects that integration. Whether he or she, Sam leads from a place that holds both structure and soul. In every Top-Down moment, they reveal what the next era of leadership demands: not just a new model, but a new presence. One that is authentic, embodied, and free.

Timeless Leadership Speaks

The insights shared in these pages didn't come solely from study or experience. They came through a deeper connection—through stillness, through listening, and trusting what could not always be seen but was always felt. They came from The BoardRoom—the voice behind this book. The BoardRoom is a sacred and intuitive space that is uniquely mine, a place where a collective of past leadership legends share their wisdom and guidance.

Their insight goes beyond knowledge or strategy alone, offering leaders a new way of seeing, choosing, and leading.

Every leader can access deeper wisdom if they are willing to trust their intuition. When we create space to listen within, we open ourselves to guidance that transcends what we already know—and that's where the next evolution of leadership begins.

One of the insights brought forward through the BoardRoom was the creation of the LEADER Archetype—a framework to help leaders grow with clarity and alignment. But more importantly, the BoardRoom shaped the spirit of this entire book: a reminder that leadership isn't just about performance. It's about presence, purpose, and connection to something greater than ourselves.

This book was built from that place—and it invites you to lead from that place, too.

What to Expect in These Pages

You'll feel the voice of the BoardRoom throughout these pages—offering insight not just about leadership, but about energy, legacy, and the lasting ripple of your influence.

This book unfolds through real stories, intuitive reflections, and the LEADER Archetype model—a framework of Six Elements that provides structure and meaning for the journey ahead. Each chapter carries a message. Some will challenge you; others will center you. But all are here to offer something deeper than technique—truth.

You won't just engage with tools; you'll activate them. These tools will ground you in who you are and sharpen how you lead in a world that demands more every day. They will push you beyond what you know, challenge the limits you've unconsciously accepted, and expand the leader you're capable of becoming.

The future won't be shaped by what you've already achieved—but by how deeply you're willing to grow, and by the leaders you have the courage to develop alongside you.

You'll explore how presence changes everything, how intuition strengthens strategic clarity, and how aligned leadership moves faster and farther than control ever could. You'll meet Sam—the CEO at the heart of these stories—and the employees alongside them, walking through real, sometimes uncomfortable moments of transformation and growth.

My Personal Invitation

Yes, this book is deeply personal.

It doesn't come only from my head; it comes from my heart—and from the BoardRoom, the voice that rises above the noise.

If you take away one thing from this book, let it be this:

You already make a difference.

But this book is also a blueprint—an invitation to lead with greater depth, clarity, and soul than ever before.

When your leadership is rooted in truth, presence, and purpose, you hold the power to transform everything around you—your team, your culture, and your legacy.

Let's lead from that place.

Transformation flows from trust, courage, alignment, and intention. ~ The BoardRoom

INTRODUCTION

The world doesn't need more leaders.
It needs more leaders who make a
difference. ~ The BoardRoom

A New Kind of Leadership

You're standing at the front of the room and all eyes are on you.

They expect vision. Answers. Confidence.

You've delivered before—bold plans, steady direction, and executive presence.

But this time, something feels different.

Beneath the polish, a quiet question arises: *Is there more?*

What if leadership isn't just about performing under pressure, but about having the courage to listen within?

What if your greatest power isn't in the answers you give, but in the questions you dare to ask?

Who This Book Is For

This book is for leaders who sense that shift—those who've mastered the external game and are now ready to lead with greater depth, clarity, and soul.

And we are at a turning point.

Leadership is no longer defined by control, charisma, or credentials. It's defined by presence, alignment, and the ability to lead from within.

The Origin of The BoardRoom

That turning point began for me in a space I call The BoardRoom.

Not the wood-paneled meeting space of corporate tradition, but a channeled, intuitive space where extraordinary wisdom flows.

The BoardRoom is a multidimensional council of visionary leaders and innovators—a dynamic collective known for its mastery of strategy, innovation, transformation, and leadership.

They don't just offer ideas—they illuminate pathways to impactful leadership. Their combined wisdom empowers me to help leaders initiate meaningful change and lead with greater purpose.

Their messages are always clear, timely, and tailored—delivered with both precision and vision.

I am the voice of The BoardRoom.

They speak through me—on every page of this book.

That is what makes this connection so distinct—and so powerful.

The Intuitive Advantage

The BoardRoom is uniquely mine. But you, too, have access to deep inner wisdom through your intuition.

Everyone has it. Whether or not you choose to access it, it's always there. Your inner guidance system: quiet, present, and powerful.

It may not speak as a council, but it speaks—with clarity, knowing, and truth.

For me, intuition is the bridge between the seen and the unseen. It allows me to receive, interpret, and act on the insights offered through The BoardRoom.

It doesn't replace logic—it completes it. It adds context to data, depth to decisions, and clarity to chaos. It transforms leadership from reactive to responsive, from habitual to intentional.

That's why I rely on it—not to override experience, but to expand it. Not to soften leadership, but to strengthen it with discernment, presence, and truth.

The Space Every Leader Needs

That's why you need a space of your own—not a BoardRoom, but a personal sanctuary.

A space where you connect with your intuitive wisdom.

A space where strategy meets soul.

Where the noise quiets and truth speaks.

Because leadership without self-connection becomes performance. But leadership with self-connection becomes transformation.

This book will help you find that place.

Why This Matters Now

Because neither strategy nor speed are enough. And success—without purpose—will never be enough.

You're leading in a world that is uncertain and divided. The pressure hasn't eased.

Yet the need for conscious, intuitive, human leadership has never been greater.

That's why *Be the Difference Now* exists.

Not to add another leadership book to your shelf—but to redefine what leadership means in a world hungry for something real.

What This Book Offers You

This isn't a book about climbing the ladder faster.

It's about reshaping the ladder entirely—so it aligns with your values, your truth, your vision.

What I share here is grounded in nearly five decades of real leadership—shaped through high-stakes decisions, hard-earned lessons, and the deep inner work that ultimately redefined how I lead—from the inside out.

I don't offer sanitized stories or recycled strategies. I offer truth through lived experiences, proven tools, and moments that cut through fear and open the door to something greater.

Because the most powerful leaders don't lead from fear—they lead from within.

Introducing the LEADER Archetype

You'll be introduced to the LEADER Archetype—a future-ready model composed of Six Elements:

- **L**ead with vision and presence.

- **E**ngage through connection, not control.
- **A**uthentic leadership that's real, not rehearsed.
- **D**eliberate action grounded in clarity.
- **E**mpower others by how you show up.
- **R**esult through the fruition of effort and intention.

You'll learn to ignite and leverage your intuition—not as a soft skill, but as a strategic edge that elevates every aspect of how you lead.

You'll deepen trust within your executive team, foster stronger collaboration, and build a culture aligned with both purpose and performance.

A Three-Lens Framework

Each chapter explores leadership through three vital lenses:

- **Sam's Top-Down Effect**—decisions viewed through a CEO's lens.
- **The Employees' Bottom-Up Effect**—how those decisions are experienced on the ground.
- **The Ripple Effect**—the unseen waves that move through your people, your culture, and your results.

Your Leadership—Your Legacy

This book is written for you—the CEO, the executive leader.

Your leadership sets the tone for everything that follows.

But this journey isn't just about achievement. It's about evolution—about who you'll become, and the difference only you can make.

Let this book be your shift.

Your signal.

Your return to what matters most.

Ask Yourself ...

- Am I proud of the leader I am when no one's watching?
- Am I inspiring others to rise?
- Will I do the right and difficult thing—even if it disrupts everything?

Because the world doesn't need more conventional leadership. It needs leaders who are aligned, aware, and unafraid to lead with soul.

Leading with soul is like trading a rigid blueprint for a compass aligned to truth—your truth.

Now is the time. This is your invitation to be the difference now.

The world doesn't need more
accomplished executives.
It needs leaders who are courageous enough
to lead with purpose. ~ The BoardRoom

Chapter 1

Derailed in the Boardroom

Your choices matter. ~ The BoardRoom

As a Chief Executive Officer (CEO), you spend countless hours selecting, developing, and investing in the right people to lead alongside you.

You train, mentor, and model the values you expect to see reflected throughout your organization. But the truth is—no amount of preparation can fully predict how someone will lead when it truly counts.

It is only in the heat of real-time decisions, during unscripted interactions and unexpected challenges, that you begin to see who is ready, who needs more support, and what kind of leadership your culture truly reflects.

Leadership in Motion

You can't control every behavior, every word, or every decision your leaders make.

What you can control is your response when those decisions don't align with the standards and values you've worked hard to build.

Leadership isn't about perfection. It's about presence.

It's about showing up in those difficult moments to coach, realign, and remind your team that leadership is a responsibility, not just a title. It's about demonstrating through your own actions that growth, accountability, and respect are non-negotiable.

Words matter. Actions matter. And the timing matters just as much.

A well-timed word of encouragement, a private correction handled with dignity, or a public show of unity after a misstep can speak volumes about the culture you're building. At the end of the day, it's not leaders over people or people over leaders—it's all of us, working together, sharing ideas, learning from mistakes, and empowering one another to create something extraordinary. Unity isn't just a concept—it's the cornerstone of every thriving organization.

Unity for the Long Haul

Once you've built alignment—when people understand the values, embrace the vision, and commit to the mission—it's tempting to ease up.

But alignment isn't a finish line. It's a daily practice.

Many leaders assume momentum will carry the culture forward. They stop having the conversations that created unity in the first place. But alignment doesn't sustain itself. It drifts in the absence of presence, trust, and follow-through.

Complacency creeps in when check-ins disappear. Trust erodes when leaders disconnect. Misalignment grows quietly—until the culture you thought was solid starts to wobble beneath the surface.

As CEO, your role isn't just to create alignment. It's to sustain it.

That means staying close—close to your leaders, your teams, and the real-time pulse of your organization. It means ensuring that relationships are as strong as strategy. That your leaders aren't just executing plans—they're building bridges, modeling values, and listening deeply to the people they serve.

When employees feel seen, heard, and supported by their leaders, they speak up sooner. They surface what's working, what's not, and what's shifting before it becomes a problem. That kind of candor isn't just good for morale—it's critical for business.

Sustained alignment lives in everyday interactions. It grows in relationships grounded in trust and strengthened through ongoing dialogue. And it shows up in how your leaders embody your vision—not just when you're in the room, but especially when you're not.

When Leadership Quietly Goes Off-Course

As CEOs, we devote significant effort to shaping culture, developing strong leaders, and creating environments where people can thrive. Yet even with the right systems in place, leadership can veer off course—not always out of malice, but sometimes from a momentary lapse in awareness, humility, or alignment.

These moments matter.

They test not only the individuals involved but the culture we've worked so hard to build. They call on us to step in—not to shame, but to reinforce what leadership truly means in our organization.

What follows is a personal account of one such moment. It began as a promising opportunity for innovation and collaboration but quickly revealed a disconnect that needed to be addressed—not just for the individuals involved, but for the health and integrity of our leadership culture.

When power is misused, trust fractures. And where trust breaks, culture reveals what leadership truly stands for. ~ The BoardRoom

Sam's Top-Down Effect

As CEO, I watched the unfolding events in the boardroom with growing unease. At my request, our top executives had gathered to hear a strategic initiative presented by one of our promising leaders. This moment had the potential to guide our company toward significant progress.

The presenter, composed and well-prepared, began outlining her team's strategy. But before Quinn could delve into the heart of her proposal, her manager—a leader on my executive team—interrupted sharply:

> "This is not what I approved," she stated, her tone not leaving any room for discussion. "We need to revisit the direction. For now, let's focus on gathering executive team feedback."

Her abruptness sent a noticeable chill through the room. I watched as the presenter's confidence faltered; her moment of leadership was derailed without warning.

Turning to Quinn, I asked, "Are you ready to continue?"

She nodded and proceeded confidently, addressing challenging questions with grace and professionalism despite her supervisor's lack of support.

After the meeting, I felt compelled to address what I had witnessed. I scheduled a private conversation with the executive who had undermined her team member.

"Your interruption during the presentation surprised me," I began. "Can you clarify your reasoning?"

She shifted uncomfortably. "I wasn't sure what she was presenting, and I needed more time to clarify."

"Had you met with her before the presentation?"

"Yes."

"Then, what needed clarifying?"

Her response did little to ease my concern. It became clear that her actions were more about control than collaboration.

"Leadership here isn't about dominance or ego," I said firmly. "It's about empowering teams, fostering trust, and leading with integrity. Publicly undermining a team member is unacceptable and counterproductive."

I emphasized the importance of cultivating an environment where leaders feel supported and valued. This incident served as a clear reminder that our leadership culture must be continuously nurtured to avoid fear-based behaviors.

In the days that followed, I led executive leadership meetings to reinforce our values and expectations. I also personally acknowledged the presenter's resilience, making sure she knew her contributions were recognized and appreciated.

This experience underscored the need for vigilant, compassionate leadership. As CEO, it's my responsibility to ensure our leadership team embodies trust, collaboration, and empowerment—and sets the tone for the entire organization.

The Employees' Bottom-Up Effect

As told by Quinn

I prepared for this day with everything I had.

My presentation was solid. My strategy was clear. I had rehearsed every word, every slide. Just yesterday, I confirmed that my manager was fully on board. I walked into that boardroom ready.

And then, just as I began, it happened.

"This is not what I approved," my boss said sharply,
her voice slicing through the room.

I froze.

She dismissed my work—*me*—in front of the entire executive team. No warning. No attempt to clarify. Just a public takedown designed to humiliate and control.

It wasn't the first time she'd undermined me. But it was the most public—and the most painful.

I stood there, breath caught in my chest, fighting to maintain composure while a thousand thoughts raced through my mind. *Why? What just happened? How am I supposed to recover from this?*

Then I heard a different voice.

"Are you prepared to continue?" Sam, our CEO, asked.

Just five words. But they shifted everything.

I took a deep breath. "Yes."

And I did. I focused not on her, but on the CEO and the other executives who were listening. The ones who were leaning in, not shutting me down. I delivered every part of that strategy just as I had practiced—professional, composed, and determined not to let one voice define the outcome.

My manager frowned through the rest of the meeting. When I finished, she quickly added, "I'll handle it from here." But her words lacked impact. The room had already heard what they needed to hear.

When I walked out, the weight of it hit me hard. Not just disappointment in her—but in the silence of the room. *Did no one else see what had just happened?* I felt exposed, discouraged, and unsure of whether I wanted to stay in a place where this could occur without anyone speaking up.

"It's time to go," I thought, opening a blank resignation draft on my laptop.

Then my phone rang. It was Sam.

My voice wavered as I answered. "Hello."

"Quinn, you did an excellent job," he said. "Your preparation was evident, and your composure under pressure speaks volumes. I want to discuss a few points further."

Then, a pause.

"I also want to acknowledge what happened in that room. You handled it with grace. I appreciate your resilience."

That moment changed everything. I had been ready to leave. But his words reminded me what real leadership looks like: direct, compassionate, accountable.

I stayed.

And in the weeks that followed, change began. Conversations happened. Expectations were clarified. Culture shifted.

I went on to have a long, fulfilling career with a company that came to value not just top-down authority, but the strength of voices from below.

Leadership isn't tested in strategy sessions,
it's revealed in moments of disruption,
when alignment, humility, and character
are needed most. ~ The BoardRoom

The Cost of Control

When leadership drifts from trust, collaboration, and alignment, quiet gaps begin to form. Sam's story illustrates how a single misstep—rooted in control rather than empowerment—can erode confidence and disrupt progress. It also reveals the power of presence, the necessity of course correction, and the importance of standing firm in your core values.

These moments point to a larger truth: the future of leadership cannot be built on outdated models of hierarchy and fear. It must evolve.

The next chapter introduces leadership reimagined—a vision for what forward-thinking leaders must now embrace. A vision rooted in authenticity, innovation, and the courage to seek solutions beyond what they already know.

What comes next isn't just a new idea—it's a new way of seeing leadership.

A model designed to move leaders from performance to presence—and from alignment to activation.

CHAPTER 2

REIMAGINING LEADERSHIP FOR A NEW ERA

*Only look back to learn—so you reshape what's
ahead with greater clarity, purpose, and intention.*
~ The BoardRoom

What if your title disappeared tomorrow—would your leadership still stand?

You weren't called here to repeat what leadership used to be. You were called to reimagine it.

Today's world is moving quickly—technology, expectations, values, and workforce dynamics are shifting all at once. Yet in many organizations, leadership hasn't kept pace.

Titles no longer earn trust. Authority doesn't automatically command respect.

Now, it's your presence that shapes outcomes. It's your alignment that sustains momentum. And the leaders we remember? They're not the ones who controlled—they're the ones who elevated.

Especially at the top. For Chief Executive Officers (CEOs), leadership isn't just a title or a task. It's infrastructure.

You set the tone. You architect the culture. You model what's allowed—and what's possible.

That's why the shift away from hierarchy and command isn't a preference—it's a pulse. It's already happening. The question is: are you responding to it—or resisting it?

From Power to Presence

Let's be clear: this isn't about softening leadership. It's about strengthening it—by anchoring it in something more whole, more human, and more real.

We're moving from:

- Dominance to discernment
- Control to coherence
- Managing people to unlocking potential
- Directing action to creating alignment

This isn't theory. It's lived truth.

Because the cultures we build don't begin in strategy decks. They're shaped in moments of presence, energy, and choice.

When authority is overused and trust is undernourished, the organization begins to fragment.

Communication breaks down. Decisions get delayed. People go quiet. And fear fills the silence.

The result?

The organization slows down—while the world speeds up.

Real Leadership Is Relational

Today's leaders aren't remembered for how much they controlled. They're remembered for how much they connected, aligned, and elevated.

The best CEOs know these two things:

1. Leadership isn't a solo sport.
2. You can't lead humans if you haven't mastered the art of being one.

It takes presence.

It takes humility.

And it takes the willingness to be shaped by the very people you lead.

That doesn't diminish your power—it expands it.

Because when you stop performing leadership and start practicing it, people stop resisting and start responding.

Redefining Leadership
Without Apology

Let's not outsource the definition of leadership to history books or business schools. Let's define it by how we embody it.

Leadership is not control. It's clarity in motion. It's the energy you carry, the tone you set, and the alignment between what you say and how you live.

It has nothing to do with your title. And everything to do with your presence.

Real leaders don't speak to impress.

They move with intention.

They listen with integrity, calibrating their field before issuing a directive.

Your role isn't just to lead. It's to recognize and activate leadership—wherever it lives.

A Crisis in Plain Sight

Most leadership breakdowns don't come from market pressures. They come from outdated models. From unexamined ego. From promoting managers over leaders.

If you want to build what's next, you have to look at what's still running on old code.

Ask yourself:

- Who on your team is still leading from fear or habit?
- Who truly lives your values—and who just recites them?
- Who unites—and who clings to control?

Culture doesn't follow your strategy. It follows your signals. And your signals come from people—not policies.

You can't architect the future with leaders anchored to the past.

Leadership in a New Landscape

Post-pandemic leadership isn't about going back. It's about moving forward—with precision and presence.

The last few years didn't just disrupt operations—they exposed truth:

- Empathy matters.
- Flexibility is strength.
- Leadership that ignores humanity won't last.

Connection is your edge—if you're willing to claim it.
The new era belongs to those who:

- Listen more deeply
- Adapt more wisely
- Lead from the inside out

Control may organize people. But inspiration moves them.

The future of leadership begins where ego ends.
~ The BoardRoom

Sam's Top-Down Effect

I've always prided myself on our team's resilience and adaptability. But nothing prepared us for the unprecedented challenges that the COVID-19 pandemic brought.

In those early days, uncertainty and fear loomed large.

Our employees were carrying invisible burdens—personal crises, illness, homeschooling, and emotional overload. It was clear: we couldn't lead the old way.

So, I gave my leaders the flexibility to support their teams as they saw fit. I encouraged empathy, listening, and humanity.

Except ... not everyone listened.

One afternoon, I overheard Tommy, one of my executive leaders, speaking sharply to Sarah, one of our most dedicated team members. Sarah had simply asked for flexibility due to school closures and her daughter being home.

Tommy's response?

"Everyone's got problems, Sarah. If you can't work your hours, maybe this isn't the place for you."

I was appalled. Not just by Tommy's words—but by his complete lack of empathy.

Sarah's situation wasn't unique. Dozens of employees were juggling work with unprecedented personal responsibilities, from caring for sick relatives to managing households during lockdown. It became evident that our leadership approach needed to evolve.

I called my executive team together. We had to shift—fast. We couldn't lead through this with old thinking. So, we formed a diverse, cross-functional team to reimagine how we work. Virtual roundtables. Mental health support. Work-from-home flexibility. Open communication.

As weeks turned into months, engagement rose, and innovation flourished. The COVID-19 crisis became the catalyst that made us rethink traditional business models.

Reflecting on this journey, I learned that true leadership isn't about having all the answers. It's about leading with empathy, embracing vulnerability, and empowering others to contribute their ideas. As The BoardRoom likes to say, "You can't have progress without change."

The Employees' Bottom-Up Effect

As told by Sarah

I didn't expect to become a catalyst for change. I wasn't even trying to. I was just trying to survive.

Like so many of my colleagues during the height of the COVID-19 pandemic, I was working full-time while trying to homeschool a seven-year-old with crayons in one hand and a spreadsheet in the other. My days were long, and my nerves were shot. But I kept showing up—loyal, tired, and doing my best.

So, I asked Tommy for a bit of flexibility,
I still remember the sting of his response.

> "This is the job, Sarah. You're either in or you're out. We all have problems—we still show up. If you can't commit to your hours, maybe this isn't the right place for you."

I felt like I'd been slapped.

I left the conversation feeling stunned and humiliated. I kept thinking: *Is this really how we lead? Is this who we are?*

What shook me even more wasn't just Tommy's tone—it was the silence that followed. I knew others had witnessed or overheard it. And yet... no one said anything.

> I remember whispering to a colleague later, "Did anyone else hear that?"

> She nodded. "We all did."

> "So, why didn't anyone step in?"

> She shrugged. "Maybe they were afraid. Maybe they thought someone else would."

Then she added quietly, "Thank God you said something."

I didn't know it at the time, but that moment with Tommy lit the fuse on something bigger.

Within days, employees began speaking up—not to tear down leadership, but to ask: "How can we lead better?"

And when Sam called an all-hands meeting shortly after, you could feel the air change.

"We heard what happened," she said. "And we're not going to let silence be the culture here. We're listening. Starting now."

She didn't deflect. She didn't protect the status quo. She acknowledged the gap between the kind of leadership we needed and what we had experienced. And just like that, the energy shifted from resignation to activation.

That moment—*our moment*—was the beginning of the bottom-up effect.

We formed virtual roundtables. Not just task forces or committees, but safe spaces where employees of all levels could share ideas and lived experiences. And Sam showed up to listen. Not to talk, not to lead—just to listen.

We weren't just asking for flexibility. We were offering solutions. A new cadence of team check-ins. Wellness days. Peer support groups. Asynchronous work models.

To Sam's credit, she didn't just tolerate these ideas—she championed them. She used her position to amplify our voices, not override them.

Looking back, it wasn't a new policy that changed our company. It was a moment of courage from the bottom up that was met with humility from the top down.

That's when I realized: leadership doesn't always wear a title. It lives in the people brave enough to speak up and the ones wise enough to listen.

True leadership isn't defined by who
speaks first, but by who listens,
who uplifts, and who dares to lead differently.
~ The BoardRoom

The Future Isn't Managed—It's Activated.

What Sarah showed wasn't rebellion. It was real-time, aligned leadership. And that's how cultures change—from the inside out.

When top-down presence meets bottom-up truth, transformation happens.

Are you building what's next—or holding on to what's been?

The next chapter introduces the LEADER Archetype—a Six Element model for the new era of leadership. It will help you lead with vision, energy, trust, and alignment—so you don't just manage culture, you become the force that shapes it.

This is your moment to awaken the future of leadership.

CHAPTER 3

THE LEADER ARCHETYPE

*Leadership impact is a direct result of
leadership integrity.* ~ The BoardRoom

Most leadership frameworks explain the past. The LEADER Archetype was built for what's next.

The world doesn't need more people in leadership roles. It needs more people who actually know how to lead—clearly, consistently, and from the inside out. The title on your business card might open a few doors, but only the energy you bring, the presence you hold, and the decisions you make will keep them open.

And Chief Executive Officers (CEOs)? You're not here to replicate what was. You're here to initiate what's never been done.

The ground beneath leadership is changing. The story is no longer about control. It's about coherence. The way we lead must catch up to the world we're actually in.

That's why we created the LEADER Archetype.

Not to give you more work. To give you something that works.

This is not a personality profile or another checklist of leadership traits.

The LEADER Archetype is a frequency-based, future-ready model for leaders who are ready to lead from truth. It is built on Six Elements that are catalytic and, together, activate a complete and aligned style of leadership that is grounded in integrity and built to last.

This framework isn't theoretical. It's transformational.

The LEADER Archetype—Six Elements of Leadership

When all Six Elements are embodied, leadership becomes fluid, congruent, and culture-shaping.

06 Result

01 Lead

The Leader Archetype

Six Elements of Leadership

05 Empower

02 Engage

04 Deliberate

03 Authentic

Lead:
Begin with integrity. Align before you act. Model what matters.

Engage:
Speak with vision. Connect through clarity. Activate belonging.

Authentic:
Be real. Be consistent. Be seen. Build trust through truth.

Deliberate:
Speak with purpose. Choose with precision. Act with impact.

Empower:
Release control. Share ownership. Elevate others.

Result:
Let impact echo intention. Lead what lasts.

The Elements aren't sequential—they're systemic.

You don't progress through them. You embody them.

When one is missing, the culture knows. When all are present, something changes.

The organization breathes easier. Trust builds faster. Growth feels different—not forced, but alive.

This is what aligned leadership feels like.

The Archetype re-centers leadership around presence—yours.

Not performance. Not pretense. Not pressure. Presence.

It aligns who you are with how you lead, so your influence is clean, your presence steady, and your culture in rhythm.

It's not another model to manage.

It's the frequency your leadership already wants to become.

Because you don't shape culture by rules. You shape it by resonance.

And the LEADER Archetype raises that resonance.

> *When the Six Elements align,*
> *leadership stops being effort and*
> *starts being transmission.* ~ The BoardRoom

Sam's Top-Down Effect

Something wasn't adding up. Steve's department had stellar performance on paper—but on the floor, the energy was flat. People avoided eye contact. Conversations died mid-sentence. I didn't see a team—I saw fear.

I sent Manny in. He's one of our best—aligned, intuitive, trusted. If something was off, he'd feel it.

He did. The moment he walked in, conversations stopped. Eyes shifted toward Steve's office. The message was clear: silence equals safety.

Then came the incident. It wasn't catastrophic, but serious enough to document. Manny followed protocol. Steve snapped—publicly berated him, then tore up the report.

That was the moment I knew: this wasn't a lapse. It was a pattern. Fear, intimidation, buried truths—and a spotless record built on deception.

I fired Steve immediately. Not just for what he did, but for what he represented: a culture of silence.

I gave Manny the team.

And slowly, the room began to breathe again.

This wasn't a personnel issue—it was a leadership fracture. Because the most dangerous leaders are the ones who look perfect on paper but lead through fear behind the scenes.

The Employees' Bottom-Up Effect

As told by Jason

Every morning, a knot twisted in our stomachs as we stepped through the doors, dreading another day under Steve's rule.

He ran the department with an iron grip. His deep, unyielding voice could silence a room before anyone even thought of speaking. He didn't need to remind us of the rules, but he did anyway:

> "Nothing leaves this department," he warned. "Anyone who talks deals with me."

We had seen what happened to those who didn't fall in line—like Kyle.

> "Did he even get a warning?" Lisa asked.

> Jason shook his head. "One day, he was here. The next, his badge didn't work."

Kyle's crime? Asking a question about safety protocols.

So, we learned. Keep your head down. Look away. Nod when Steve twists the truth. Our silence kept food on our tables and roofs over our heads.

Then Manny showed up.

Manny was different. He asked real questions. He listened. He looked us in the eye.

"What's the biggest challenge you face in your day-to-day work?" he asked, his expression open, curious.

Jason muttered, "Depends on who's asking."

Manny sighed. "I'm asking."

For a moment, it felt like maybe—just maybe—someone was finally here to fix things.

Then Steve made his move.

"You're getting a little too comfortable, Manny," he said, his voice low, laced with warning.

Manny met his gaze. "I'm trying to understand how things work around here."

Steve stepped closer. "Things work just fine. If you've got a problem with that, there's the door."

His gaze swept over us, daring anyone to speak. No one did.

After that, we avoided Manny, kept our heads down, and nodded along when Steve twisted the truth.

Then it happened.

Lisa burst into the breakroom; face drained of color. "The conveyor line …" she gasped. "Just like we warned Steve. Only—" She swallowed hard, her voice barely above a whisper. "No one warned *him*."

We all knew what she meant. It never would've happened if Steve had cared about fixing the problem instead of covering it up.

This time, Manny didn't look away. He documented everything. He confronted Steve and stood his ground.

Jason sighed. "How much you wanna bet Manny's badge won't work tomorrow?"

"Yeah," Lisa muttered. "Steve will fire him. Just like all the others."

Then, the announcement came:

"Effective immediately, Steve has been removed from his position."

Silence.

Mark let out a low whistle. "Holy cow. Manny did it!"

For the first time in years, we exhaled—releasing the fear and resignation we hadn't realized we'd been holding. In its place, something new stirred: hope.

It took time for us to trust that things had changed and to find our voices again. But as the days passed, we did.

And for the first time in years, work didn't feel like survival. It felt like what it should have been all along—a place of growth, collaboration, and safety.

Each Element of the LEADER Archetype is a facet of the whole. Only by embodying them all do you represent the leadership the future demands.
~ The BoardRoom

What Comes Next

You've seen what misaligned leadership costs—the burnout, the breakdowns, the culture that runs on empty. And you've felt the toll of disconnection, the drag of misalignment, the gap between intention and impact.

Now, it's time to step into what aligned leadership truly requires: presence, clarity, and the courage to lead from the inside out.

What comes next isn't a better version of the old model—It's a recalibration of how leadership moves through you, and how that movement shapes everything around you.

In the next chapter, we begin with the first Element—Lead—not as a function, but as a frequency. You'll explore why presence, values, and alignment are no longer optional for CEOs. They're your foundation.

PART I
L IS FOR LEAD

Welcome to Part I.

The first Element of the LEADER Archetype begins with the foundation: Lead. These chapters explore what it truly means to lead, not from title, but from alignment. This section consists of three chapters, each designed to help Chief Executive Officers (CEOs) and executive leaders examine how they lead themselves, how they lead through alignment, and how they lead others with presence, conviction, and integrity.

We begin by looking inward, reconnecting with the internal compass that guides authentic decision-making. Next, we move toward strategic alignment—ensuring that personal clarity and organizational direction advance together. Finally, we explore how leadership presence is maintained not just by performance, but through nourishment, reflection, and intentional modeling.

Together, these chapters challenge the notion that leadership is an isolated, outward endeavor. Instead, they invite us to consider how our inner and outer selves, as a complete package, influence the way we lead.

Let's begin.

CHAPTER 4

LEAD FROM THE POWER WITHIN

Mirrors share more than an image. ~ The BoardRoom

Most CEOs don't become leaders through strategy. They become leaders in a moment—a decision, a pause, or a test of integrity. When alignment mattered more than approval, and presence mattered more than control. That's when leadership stops being a role—and becomes who you are.

Every accomplished leader eventually confronts this truth:

You can only lead others as deeply as you are willing to lead yourself.

Everything else—strategy, execution, influence—flows from that foundation. Without it, leadership becomes hollow, reactive, and performative.

Leadership doesn't start with authority or direction. It begins with the discipline of self-reflection—knowing who you are, what you stand for, and how your presence influences the energy around you.

Without clarity, courage, and alignment with your values, even the best-designed strategies will falter under pressure—and teams will struggle to fully commit.

This truth doesn't arrive in a training—it reveals itself through experience.

A Defining Decision

A rising executive faced a defining moment during a high-stakes board meeting. A respected partner proposed a lucrative pivot: abandon the company's long-term vision in exchange for short-term gains. The market would celebrate. Rewards would come swiftly. But accepting the proposal meant betraying the company's core values—and the commitments made to employees and stakeholders alike.

The room fell silent. The choice wasn't about business anymore—it was about principle. Would they hold alignment or yield to pressure?

They stayed the course. Integrity prevailed over approval. Vision took precedence over volatility.

That choice became a legacy moment—not because of the applause after, but because of the silence they endured. The BoardRoom upholds:

> Real leadership is forged in these moments. It's in the silence where truth is loudest—and where alignment either holds or breaks.

A Lesson in Influence

Leadership begins where few are watching—in the quiet, everyday moments that test our awareness.

Influence isn't one-directional—it's an exchange. As a leader, you don't just shape the room; the room shapes you. What you allow in—emotionally, mentally, energetically—determines what you reflect out. And if you're not intentional about that, you're leading by default, not by design.

One evening, a seasoned CEO noticed rising tension within their body—a clenched jaw, a tight stomach, a dull ache. Nothing had happened, yet something felt off.

The culprit? A television in the next room echoing a biased news broadcast. It sounded informative—but it was designed to divide. And it worked—without permission.

That moment sparked a deeper realization: influence leaks are real.

They create subtle breaches in energetic clarity—slipping into your awareness uninvited and shifting your presence without your consent. Left unchecked, they erode clarity.

They show up everywhere in an organization—through unspoken norms, casual remarks, or unchecked energy. They don't just distract. They disconnect.

Even the most grounded leaders can drift off course—not because they made a wrong move, but because they absorbed the wrong signal. The BoardRoom emphasizes:

> Policy sets the rule. Consciousness gives it soul. Without both, leadership becomes either rigid or reckless—bound by control or lost in chaos. It's the union of structure and awareness that gives leadership its true strength.

Leadership begins with the choice to stay conscious, the discipline to discern what to allow in, and in the power to redirect what does not serve you.

This is more than self-awareness. This is leadership by design.

Reflection Leads to Learning

Leadership is not a title. It's a practice. A renewal. A choice.

Every pressure, every moment of influence, asks the same question: "Who is leading you?" And The BoardRoom answers:

> If you do not take charge of your mind, someone—or something—else will. If you don't define your values, you will default to someone else's. If you do not pause to choose, you will be swept into reaction. And in that reaction, you are no longer leading—you are being led.

Leadership driven by fear, convenience, or validation is unstable.

Leadership grounded in truth, clarity, and inner alignment is unshakable.

> *If you don't lead your own mind, someone else will.*
> *And once you hand over that power, everything*
> *you lead starts shifting with it.* ~ The BoardRoom

Sam's Top-Down Effect

It happened in the hallway near the Operations wing—one of those ordinary moments that changes everything.

I witnessed a highly respected executive—someone I had personally mentored—breach one of our most crucial safety protocols. It wasn't deliberate. Stan probably saw it as a small shortcut to save time.

But here's the truth: intent doesn't excuse impact. Not in leadership. Not when others are watching.

If I let it slide, I wouldn't just be ignoring the issue—I'd be giving it silent permission. And permission, especially from the top, spreads fast.

So, I made one of the hardest decisions of my career—I fired Stan. Not for optics. For integrity.

Leadership requires a wider perspective. It's not about personal preferences or past contributions—it's about the signals we send in the here and now.

And what happened next confirmed the ripple.

Managers began to reinforce expectations, and employees found their voices. Accountability didn't increase out of fear, but from clarity. Our culture didn't shatter—it sharpened.

That moment reminded me that I wasn't leading from a title—I was leading from alignment.

And if you can't lead yourself when it's hard, you have no business leading others.

Employees' Bottom-Up Effect

As told by Jordan

I used to believe leadership lived at the top—delivered through polished memos, strategy decks, and quarterly pep talks.

But the day our director was let go for breaking a safety policy, that belief shattered—in the best possible way.

Let me back up.

That director, Stan, was someone I respected. He was a real "people person." He remembered birthdays, asked about our kids, and stayed late when projects ran long. He wasn't just liked—he was trusted.

So, when I found out he'd been dismissed, I was stunned.

I overheard it being talked about in the breakroom:

"Stan bypassed the safety protocol last week—The CEO made the call herself."

I didn't want to believe it.

But leadership addressed it directly in a team meeting. It wasn't gossip. It was a line drawn—boldly and unapologetically. Still, I found myself torn between my respect for Stan and his breach of safety protocol.

At lunch, I turned to my colleague Shay, "Do you think it was necessary to fire Stan for one mistake?"

She paused. "Yes. It wasn't just about the mistake. It was about what would've happened if no one did anything."

That landed hard.

Later, a message from our CEO hit my inbox. It wasn't cold or defensive—it was honest. Sam acknowledged the difficulty with the decision. Not to make an example of someone, but to set an example *for* all of us.

"We don't uphold our values selectively," Sam wrote. "Leadership begins with how we lead ourselves—especially when no one's watching."

That stuck with me.

This wasn't about protocol anymore. It was about trust. About whether the values meant something—or were just posters on the wall.

That week, something shifted.

Managers became more consistent. People spoke up sooner. Even I started checking my own behavior—not out of fear, but out of respect. I didn't want to be the person who made it okay to look the other way.

That's when I realized: leadership isn't granted by a title—it's activated by a decision.

Insights from The BoardRoom

Most leaders are trained to focus outward—on metrics, milestones, and momentum. But true impact begins inward.

If your inner world is noisy, reactionary, or compromised, your leadership will reflect that.

Self-leadership isn't a soft skill. It's the energetic backbone of every choice, every conversation, every culture you build.

When you hold yourself accountable at the highest standard—especially when no one is watching—you establish the energetic floor for your organization. And that floor either lifts others or leaves them uncertain.

What you tolerate becomes your culture. What you confront becomes your standard.

Decisive leadership isn't about harshness. It's about clarity.

When a leader acts in alignment—even in hard moments—it signals that culture isn't a slogan. It's a standard.

Conscious leadership turns difficult decisions into realignments. It clarifies values. It redirects energy. It rebuilds trust.

Self-leadership isn't about perfection. It's about alignment. And from alignment comes power, clarity, and trust.

Lead with Alignment—Not Effort

Leadership doesn't start with others—it begins within. When you lead yourself first, you set the tone for how you influence, decide, and show up. This chapter grounded us in the power of self-alignment, the clarity of inner leadership, and the personal responsibility required to lead from truth.

From here, we move deeper into reflection—not just on what you do, but how your presence shapes the space around you.

In the next chapter, we'll explore how to project that inner leadership outward—through the lens of clarity and conscious presence. You'll meet the *Leadership Mirror*, a practice that doesn't just reveal who you are, but shows you how your presence shapes everything around you.

CHAPTER 5

THE LEADERSHIP MIRROR

The clearest sign of leadership isn't what others see in you—it's what you're willing to see in yourself. ~ The BoardRoom

In leadership, the most obvious truths are often the easiest to overlook.

For CEOs, the relentless drive to perform, respond, and anticipate can create a forward-leaning posture—always forecasting, always scanning the horizon. But that same instinct can blur what's most essential: seeing yourself with clarity.

The most transformational leaders don't just lead—they examine themselves first. And understand that leadership presence is a reflection of inner alignment.

If your team seems reactive, disengaged, or confused, the first place to look isn't the strategy deck—it's the mirror.

Not the one that reflects your title, your results, or your curated image. The one that reveals your intentions, your unspoken energy, your unfiltered influence.

That's the Leadership Mirror.

Presence Over Performance

A leader walks into the room. No announcement. No agenda. Yet the energy shifts.

Why? Because presence speaks before words do.

Presence is more than body language or tone of voice. It's the emotional atmosphere you carry—the frequency you set without saying a word.

And your team can feel it.

Your presence is shaped by:

- The emotions you carry.
- The energy you avoid.
- The truth you haven't resolved.

Self-reflection isn't soft—it's a power move. It turns awareness into impact.

When you reflect daily—not on what you did, but on what you brought—you become a leader of resonance, not just results.

And that resonance? It starts before you say a single word.

Subtle Cues. Loud Impact

Consider this: You walk into a meeting after a heated board call. You smile, greet the team, and dive in.

On the surface, everything looks fine. But your energy got there first.

And if you were still simmering from the call, your tension walked in ahead of you. That smile? That upbeat tone? They don't match.

The disconnect is subtle—but your team feels it. And they tighten, hesitate, and filter what they hear.

They're not reacting to what you said. They're reacting to how you showed up. This is the invisible side of leadership—the influence of unspoken signals. As The BoardRoom reminds us:

> Your tone sets the tone. What you praise, others prioritize. Where you focus, others follow. And what you ignore, silently teaches them what doesn't matter.

Now flip the mirror.

What are your team's subtle cues telling you?

If feedback is delayed, trust is uncertain, or decisions stall—your people may be responding not to your leadership, but to your lack of presence.

Leadership requires the courage to see in yourself what you ask others to follow.

The Leadership Mirror isn't a tool—it's a threshold.
It's where ego meets truth, and performance
meets presence.
It's not where leadership is performed—it's where
leadership is remembered.
~ The BoardRoom

Sam's Top-Down Effect

There's a moment I think about often. In some ways, it haunts me.

I was in the middle of a major turnaround—high pressure, high stakes, constant motion. I told myself I was holding it together. But my team knew better.

One day, after a particularly tense strategy session, I pulled my team together to check in. I focused on the facts, trying to keep my words and tone upbeat.

We weren't far into the meeting when my Chief of Staff pulled me aside and said, "What is bothering you? You're off today."

I started to defend myself when she said, "You don't need to say anything. Everyone can feel it. We're matching you. We're matching your energy."

That stopped me in my tracks.

They weren't matching my words. They were matching my worry.

Without realizing it, I'd been broadcasting doubt while trying to project confidence. And my team—loyal, capable, invested—mirrored me.

The result?

Decision-making slowed. Initiative waned. Meetings became cautious, with less candor and more second-guessing.

Their performance didn't dip due to lack of skill or effort—it was my unspoken anxiety setting the tone.

So, I paused, took space, and shifted my energy. Not by pretending to be calm, but by addressing the real tension inside. I recalibrated my practices. I reflected, not reacted.

And as I shifted, so did they.

That's when I learned: Culture doesn't start with policy. It starts with presence.

Employees' Bottom-Up Effect

As told by Melissa

I've worked under five different CEOs in my career. Some were brilliant strategists. Others, magnetic speakers. But the ones who left the biggest mark? They were the ones willing to look in the mirror and see themselves.

Sam, my current CEO, stands out.

She always says the right things—her tone is measured; her updates are sharp. But recently, something's been off. There's this tension that enters the room before she does. You can't quite put your finger on it, but you feel it.

> I remember whispering to my colleague Dan after one meeting, "Did you notice how quiet it got when Sam walked in?"
>
> He nodded. "Yeah. It's like we're all holding our breath."

At first, I chalked it up to stress. The pressure at the top is real. But then came the moment that changed everything.

Mid-sentence during a leadership meeting, Sam paused. She looked around the room, took a slow breath, and said:

> Okay. I need to name something. I've been tense. Distracted. And I know I'm bringing that energy into the room. You're not imagining it—I can feel it, too.

Her admission was met with total silence. Then, someone across the table broke it, saying:

"Thanks for saying that."

She didn't spin it. She didn't blame the workload or pivot to the agenda. She just owned it.

From that day on, the energy shifted. The room felt safer. People opened up more. Conversations became more honest. Decisions came easier.

> A week later, over lunch, Dan said, "That last meeting felt human."

> "Yeah," I said. "It's like we can finally say the hard things without worrying we'll be shut down."

Most of us don't expect perfection from our leaders. But we do hope they're doing the inner work.

Because when a leader looks in the mirror, we don't just follow orders—we trust the direction.

Insights from The BoardRoom

> The mirror doesn't lie. But it doesn't shame either. It simply reflects.

> Many leaders avoid the mirror out of fear—of what they'll see, of what they'll have to change. But the mirror is not the threat. Disconnection is.

> Your people aren't asking you to be perfect. They're asking you to be present.

They want your clarity, not just your direction. They want to follow energy that's honest, not masked in management speak.

The mirror doesn't weaken leadership—it grounds it. It earns trust without saying a word. It projects confidence without posturing. And it shifts culture without needing permission.

Once you're clear in the mirror, the next question becomes: Are you aligned in action?

Because when the mirror reflects honesty, trust becomes a natural response.

From Reflection to Alignment

When leaders are willing to face the mirror and align their presence, everything changes. Because the mirror calls for congruence.

What your people need most is your authenticity.

When your energy, intent, and actions reflect a clear internal compass, trust takes root. Culture shifts. Leadership becomes a presence with purpose.

When the mirror reflects alignment, your leadership becomes the culture your people feel first.

In the next chapter, we'll explore how aligned leadership connects vision, values, and choices when making daily decisions. Because leadership is sustained by living what you say you believe.

CHAPTER 6

ALIGN TO LEAD

What if the way you've always led is exactly what's holding you back? ~The BoardRoom

Leaders today don't suffer from a lack of strategy—they suffer from a lack of alignment.

Vision lives on the wall. Values hide in a deck. But day-to-day decisions tell the real story.

Too often, organizations move fast without pausing to ask: "Do our actions reflect our principles?"

And too often, leaders lead on autopilot—until misalignment breaks trust, derails momentum, or exposes a gap they didn't realize had widened. The BoardRoom reminds us:

> Vision isn't strategy—it's a promise. Alignment is how you keep it. Every decision either honors that promise or slowly dissolves it.

When alignment breaks down, it doesn't always make a sound.

At first, it looks like delay.

Then confusion.

Then contradiction.

Eventually, it erodes something far more difficult to repair: trust.

You don't have to say "This doesn't matter" for your team to stop prioritizing it. You just have to act in ways that don't align with it.

When decisions contradict the vision …

When actions don't mirror values …

When what's tolerated clashes with what's claimed …

Your team notices. And they stop listening to the words and start following the real signals.

Your team doesn't follow your vision.
They follow your alignment with it.
~ The BoardRoom

Sam's Top-Down Effect

I thought we were aligned.

The offsite went well—at least, that's what it looked like. We had clarity. We had buy-in. And my leadership team left the room nodding in agreement around our renewed vision: a culture built on inclusion, integrity, and intentional growth.

I believed we were solid—until a quiet conversation unraveled it all.

My head of operations asked for a one-on-one. Nothing urgent, she said—just a check-in. But the moment we sat down, I could feel a different energy.

> "Sam," she began, "I support the direction you laid out. I want it to succeed. But I'm struggling with something."

45

She paused.

> "It doesn't fully line up. What we're saying and what
> we're doing … it's not the same."

She pointed to our metrics—they still rewarded speed over depth. She referenced how we'd handled the last restructuring—efficient, yes, but missing the care we claimed to prioritize. And most importantly, she shared how her own team was beginning to feel the disconnect between our words and our actions.

She wasn't being combative. She was being honest.

And in that moment, I had a choice: defend the plan—or look in the mirror.

I chose the mirror.

What I saw wasn't failure. It was misalignment—subtle, unintentional, but deeply influential. We hadn't abandoned our vision, but we hadn't fully embodied it either.

So, I brought the conversation to the rest of the executive team. We re-examined how we measured success, how we navigated change, and how aligned we were in practice—not just in principle.

That one conversation didn't weaken our vision.

It recalibrated our leadership—together.

Employees' Bottom-Up Effect

As told by Marcus

I've been with this company for nine years. Long enough to watch leaders cycle through, visions launch and quietly fade, and culture campaigns that start with a bang and end in silence.

But after the last leadership offsite, something shifted. And it wasn't what they *said*—it was what they refused to ignore.

Sam's calendar invite landed in our inbox: "Leadership Alignment Roundtable." No slides. No pre-read. Just a question that changed everything: *"Where are we out of sync?"*

I showed up expecting spin. Instead, Sam opened with this:

> We've created a gap between what we say and what we reinforce. We're out of sync—and I want to know where you see it.

That stopped me.

Most leaders ask for feedback, then brace for the safest version of the truth. But this felt different.

When it was my turn, I paused, then said:

> We talk a lot about intentional growth. But last quarter, three people on my team were passed over for development opportunities because we were racing to hit numbers. I don't think it was intentional. But it was real.

The room went still.

Sam didn't flinch. He nodded and said:

> "You're right. That's a gap—and I take responsibility. Growth can't be a value we reference. It must be a priority we live."

And he meant it.

In the following weeks, things changed. Development time started showing up in the metrics—right alongside delivery deadlines. A mid-year growth review was reinstated. And managers weren't just asked what they were working on—but how those efforts aligned with our values.

That's when it clicked: Alignment isn't about being perfect—it's about being *willing* to correct course when you're not.

And when leadership chooses alignment, the rest of us stop guessing what matters.

We feel it.

We believe it.

And more importantly—we match it.

Insights from The BoardRoom

Vision isn't strategy. It's a promise. And alignment is how you keep it.

The most trusted leaders don't just speak their values—they sequence them into how decisions are made, how priorities are set, and how people are treated. Alignment is where values meet behavior, and where intention becomes integrity.

When leaders rush to execute before aligning internally, they unknowingly broadcast confusion. Their teams may comply, but they won't commit. That's not resistance—it's misalignment.

Culture doesn't break all at once—it drifts. Quietly. Subtly. Energetically.

It happens when feedback is delayed. When pressure overrides principle. When small misalignments go unaddressed because they're "not a big deal."

But every unspoken contradiction weakens trust.

Alignment isn't about everyone agreeing—it's about everyone believing that what's said, what's done, and what's rewarded are in sync.

This requires more than communication. It requires courage. Because to realign, you must first admit what's out of line.

The leaders of tomorrow are already listening. They're asking: "Do I trust what I see? Or just what I'm told?"

Give them your truth—not your polish.

Beyond the Mirror

You've met the first leader—yourself. You've clarified your vision. You've faced the mirror. You've chosen alignment over appearance. Now, the invitation deepens—from self-leadership to shared resonance.

But leadership doesn't live in isolation. It's revealed—in every meeting, every moment, every relationship. Because alignment alone can't transform an organization. Connection does. Trust does. Engagement does.

In Part II, E Is for Engage, you'll discover how the energy you hold either opens the door—or closes it—for others to step forward, speak up, and commit fully.

It's time to lead through presence, not pressure.

PART II
E IS FOR ENGAGE

Welcome to Part II.

Leadership begins within—but it cannot stay there.

Once you know who you are—once your values, energy, and intent are aligned—the next step is inevitable: you engage.

Engage is the second Element of the LEADER Archetype. It represents the bridge between personal clarity and collective influence. When you lead from alignment, you don't chase people—you attract them. You don't command momentum—you invite it.

Engagement is how the clarity you've cultivated internally becomes the force that draws others forward. Through your presence, example, and energetic integrity, others begin to rise alongside you.

This section explores how presence becomes progress, how trust builds momentum, and how the energy you carry as a leader radiates outward—shaping culture, elevating performance, and expanding impact.

If alignment is your foundation, engagement is the force that builds what lasts.

Let's begin.

CHAPTER 7

THE ENGAGEMENT EFFECT

Presence isn't a luxury. It is the lever
that lifts culture, unlocks energy,
and ignites engagement. ~ The BoardRoom

What if the missing link between your strategy and your success isn't performance—but presence?

In a world wired for speed and scale, too many organizations overlook the subtle force that holds everything together: engagement.

Not the program. Not the initiative. But the pulse of your people—the rhythm of how they engage, connect, contribute, and care.

We've measured engagement through dashboards, surveys, and town halls. But here's the deeper truth: engagement isn't just what employees give you—it's what leadership creates in the room.

It's a reflection of how people feel—about the mission, about themselves, and about you.

If your team feels exhausted, misaligned, or quiet, it's not a problem to fix—it's a signal to listen.

The Leadership Frequency

Presence is the true source of power. When leaders show up grounded, aware, and connected, they invite the same from others. You can't scale presence, but you can model it. You can create space for it. You can choose it. The BoardRoom reminds us:

> You cannot ask for what you do not embody.
> When presence becomes your practice, engagement becomes your legacy.
>
> The most engaged cultures don't chase energy—they cultivate it. They remove what blocks it, they listen for what fuels it, and they honor the humanity that drives it.

Engagement begins not with a program—but with a presence.

The most resonant cultures aren't energized by slogans or metrics—they're nurtured by consistency, care, and connection. What leaders prioritize, others replicate.

If you want to build engagement, lead from your energy, not just your agenda.

Presence sets the tone. Attunement holds the room. And trust builds the rhythm.

> *Engagement is the echo of your leadership*
> *frequency. When the signal is clear,*
> *people move with you. When it's fractured,*
> *they hesitate.* ~ The BoardRoom

Sam's Top-Down Effect

I walked into the break room expecting brief hellos and casual greetings. Instead, the room went silent. I had stumbled into a conversation I wasn't meant to hear.

> Everyone froze. And then, a manager broke the silence: "We're tired of being talked at."

That moment didn't feel like feedback—it felt like a reckoning. It caught me completely off guard.

It was humbling. And it was telling.

I'd been managing the culture from a distance, trusting my executive team to stay close to the ground. But now it was clear—I had made a significant mistake. I needed to engage directly.

So, I did. I stayed in the room that day—attuned, involved, and listening with empathy.

Then I paused our plans and began asking a different set of questions—not about performance, but about presence. I invited people in—not to fix things, but to co-create. I started walking the halls again—not to be seen, but to see.

We built an environment for honest dialogue—not just anonymous surveys.

Engagement didn't come from a mandate; it returned through genuine presence and shared purpose.

Bit by bit, the energy began to shift. People leaned in—and I did too. The culture responded. Not to a program, but to presence.

Engagement isn't reignited by mandates; it's rekindled by genuine presence and a shared purpose.

Employees' Bottom-Up Effect

As told by Marlene

I've been in this industry for over thirty years—and in this company for the last twelve. Long enough to know that most "culture resets" sound better in a slide deck than they feel in real life.

So, when Sam announced a new approach to engagement I admit—I rolled my eyes.

But what unfolded next was a pleasant surprise.

Sam didn't launch a program. He showed up—alone. No entourage. No talking points. Just Sam, a legal pad, and a single question: "Where are we out of sync—and what would it take to realign?"

That stopped me.

Not because the question was new but because Sam actually waited for someone to answer.

> I spoke up a little cautiously. "We talk a lot about valuing people over productivity. But for the last two quarters, all I've seen rewarded is speed. People are burning out."
>
> Sam didn't flinch. "That's the kind of truth I need to hear," he said. "Thank you for saying it."

He didn't get defensive. He didn't justify or deflect. He stayed grounded, fully present—and took it in.

And something shifted.

> A week later, my department manager opened our meeting with a question I hadn't heard in years:

"What's one thing we could stop doing that would make your work more sustainable?"

Wow, I thought, as we all started contributing ideas.

Together, we eliminated two redundant reports that had been adding unnecessary strain and added two flex hours each week—giving everyone a little more breathing room. Best of all? Leadership didn't just listen and move on. They followed through, made the changes happen, and checked back to make sure they were working.

I've seen leaders talk about change. I've rarely seen one listen—and then *make* the change.

And as a result, we stopped holding our breath. We started speaking our truth. We supported each other in a way that felt like ... *reconnected.*

Engagement isn't a pep rally—it's a pulse.

And when leadership starts listening from the heart, that pulse gets stronger. People don't just show up—they plug in. They bring their whole selves to the table, contributing not just skills and expertise, but perspective, passion, and presence.

That's what builds a vibrant, supportive culture. And it's a pulse we're all responsible for sustaining.

Insights from The BoardRoom

Engagement is not a metric—it's a living rhythm. One that rises and falls with your presence.

When leaders step into a room fully attuned—not to control, but to connect—they shift the entire frequency of the space. That shift is felt. It tells your people: *I'm here, and I see you.*

Presence outperforms policy every time.

It's easy to craft engagement statements, post values on the wall, or launch another new initiative. But people don't engage because of what's written. They engage because of what's modeled—consistently and quietly—by those who lead.

The energy of a team doesn't lie.
It's either building or breaking. Deepening or retreating.
And that energy follows where the leader places their focus.

If you prioritize results at the cost of resonance, you may hit the goal—but lose the people.

Engagement is not your goal—it's your mirror.

It reflects how aligned your leadership is with your values, how clearly your culture echoes your intentions, and how safe people feel bringing their full selves to work.

When disconnection shows up, it's not a fault—it's a frequency check.

If you're seeing detachment or fatigue, don't rush to fix it—be willing to feel it.

Behind every disengaged employee is a story. And more often than not, it's not about the work. It's about trust:

- Trust in your consistency.
- Trust in your care.
- Trust that their voice matters as much as your vision.

The greatest shift happens when you stop performing engagement and begin embodying it.

That means listening without trying to fix, staying present when silence feels uncomfortable, and trusting that what arises in those spaces holds the very intelligence your strategy is missing.

The engagement effect isn't sparked by charisma or clever programs. It's the natural outcome of presence, alignment, and follow-through.

When those are real, people don't just comply—they commit. Not because they have to—but because they want to.

You can't mandate engagement—but you can invite it.
Not with a speech—but with your presence.

That's where leadership begins to breathe again.

Presence is the Missing Link

Engagement isn't a program—it's a presence. It's not measured by how often leaders speak, but by how fully they show up.

What often separates strategy from success isn't a lack of effort—it's a lack of energetic connection. When leaders lead with presence, they unlock more than performance—they awaken participation. And when that happens? Culture starts to speak back.

In the next chapter, we shift from being visible to becoming receptive—to what your culture is trying to tell you, and what it's been waiting for you to hear. Because listening isn't just a skill—it's the clearest proof of whether your leadership is real or just for show.

CHAPTER 8

CULTURE LISTENS

A culture that truly listens never needs to shout.
~ The BoardRoom

What if the loudest voice in your company isn't yours—but the one you've been too busy to hear?

Every CEO wants an engaged culture. But culture doesn't rise from command—it grows from what you're willing to accept. If your people believe their voice matters, they will give more than compliance. They'll offer commitment.

But if they sense you only listen when it's convenient—or only to those who echo your views—they'll quietly withdraw. And your culture will follow.

Listening Is the Foundation of Unity

Leadership isn't a megaphone—it's a tuning fork.

The best leaders don't tear teams apart looking for problems—they unify rooms to uncover what's real. And listening only works when it's clear. The BoardRoom asserts:

You can't build unity while clinging to bias. Letting go isn't weakness—it's wisdom. Bias blocks the very connection you're trying to create. It narrows the lens, distorts the signal, and silences voices that would strengthen you. Letting go doesn't mean abandoning values—it means releasing filters, assumptions, and the comfort of sameness.

Unity doesn't require agreement; it requires belonging. Only a wise leader makes room for difference without fear.

Signal vs. Noise

Too many leaders confuse volume with value. If your team feels the need to raise their voices just to be heard, the real issue isn't volume—it's trust. The BoardRoom reminds us:

> If people have to shout, you've already taught them whispering isn't safe. And when whispering isn't safe, truth gets edited. Insight hides behind silence. Innovation waits in the wings, unsure if it's welcome.

This isn't about who speaks the loudest—it's about whether your leadership has made it safe for people to speak at all.

A reactive culture rewards the noise of defensiveness. A trusted culture makes room for quiet brilliance. And the voices your company needs most? They're not missing—they're just still deciding if it's worth the risk to be real.

That's not a culture flaw—it's a listening flaw. Change the signal, and the voices return.

Listening Is a Strategic Skill

This isn't just about emotional intelligence—it's about operational capacity.

Organizations that listen respond faster, solve deeper, and connect longer. When your people feel heard, they contribute—not just to the work, but to the mission.

Listening reveals what your dashboards can't. It shows you where the signal is off—*before* it costs you trust.

And here's what matters most to you, right now: Listening isn't just about morale—it's about momentum.

When employees feel heard, engagement rises, creativity flows, and decisions land stronger. When they don't, risk creeps in quietly. Blind spots grow. Performance becomes guesswork. What looks like disengagement is often unheard intelligence.

Real leaders don't just listen better—they listen sooner.

Pause to Listen Within

Leadership is as much about what you're willing to hear as what you say.

Let's take a moment—just you—and ask:

- Who in your organization is speaking, but still not being heard?
- Where has feedback become filtered, edited, or avoided?

- What parts of your culture feel inclusive—and what parts still feel guarded?

This isn't about judgment. It's about noticing. Because the moment you start listening differently, your entire culture begins to shift.

Culture isn't shaped by what leaders say—it's shaped by what they're willing to hear. Listening is not passive. It's how leadership earns the right to lead. ~ The BoardRoom

Sam's Top-Down Effect

I believed we had a listening culture—until someone told me they didn't feel safe speaking.

At first, I wanted to defend our efforts: the open-door policy, the town halls, the anonymous surveys. But then it hit me—listening isn't just about having systems in place. It's about what those systems *signal*.

The harder truth? I had been listening selectively. I heard mostly from voices that mirrored mine—people who thought like me and validated my instincts. I wasn't uncomfortable enough to notice whose voice was missing.

That changed during a leadership roundtable. A junior manager paused and quietly said, "I'm not sure my voice matters here—it never really has."

That moment didn't just sting; it woke me up.

I realized I had been seeking input but rewarding agreement. I had made space—but not made it safe.

So I changed.

I began inviting silence in meetings, letting pauses linger without rushing to fill them. I started asking, "Who else needs to weigh in before we move forward?" I gave voices time to emerge—not on my timeline, but on theirs.

Slowly, things began to shift. Not just in tone—but in trust.

People may not remember if you agreed with them, but they will remember if you listened. And when people truly feel heard, they start telling you the truths that can change everything.

Employees' Bottom-Up Effect

As told by Malcolm

I've been here almost eight years. By now I know the difference between leadership going through the motions—and leadership that actually means it.

So, when Sam announced a "listening tour," I thought, *Yeah, sure. Another PR stunt. He'll pop in, jot down a few notes, and then it's back to business as usual.*

Still, I showed up. Not out of hope—out of curiosity.

> Sam pulled up a chair, looked around, and said, "I'm here to listen. No defending. Just listening."

At first, people played it safe—surface-level stuff. But then Carla spoke.

> "I'll be honest," she said. "It doesn't feel like our voices matter. Decisions are made behind closed doors. We're not part of the process—and even now, it doesn't feel safe to say that out loud."

The room froze. Everyone braced for impact.

> But Sam didn't flinch. He nodded and said, "You're right. We haven't been listening—and that's made it feel risky to speak up."

This moment of leadership accountability was a game-changer. Sam was genuinely interested in understanding our perspective.

> So, I leaned forward and added, "Sometimes it feels like the only voices being heard are the ones that already agree. If we speak up with a different view, it goes nowhere."

> Sam looked right at me and said, "Thank you for saying that. That's exactly the kind of honesty I've been missing."

After that, it snowballed. People opened up—about broken systems, ignored ideas, and the exhaustion of constantly adjusting without context.

To Sam's credit, he didn't interrupt, defend, or deflect. He just stayed present.

> At our next department meeting, he opened with, "I've been thinking a lot about what you shared. Listening doesn't mean much if it doesn't lead to action. You trusted me with the truth. Now it's on me to enact change."

That landed. Not as a soundbite—but as truth.

Because when leaders truly listen—not to manage perception, but to understand—something in the culture realigns. And trust becomes the new frequency.

Insights from The BoardRoom

Listening is more than a skill. It's the way a culture functions:

- A listening leader creates the conditions for trust.
- A listening team creates the rhythm of progress.
- A listening organization creates belonging at scale.

Here's the truth many leaders miss: Silence isn't absence—it's data. And the quieter your people get, the more you should pay attention.

So, start again.
Be still longer.
Let discomfort teach you what familiarity never will.

The cultures that will lead the future are not those that shout the loudest—but those that are willing to listen where others won't.

Listening is Leadership

Culture isn't what you declare—it's what you demonstrate.

It lives in what you allow, encourage, and repeat. At the heart of it is one undeniable signal: how leadership listens.

Not just whether voices feel safe, seen, and heard—but whether they believe they matter.

A culture that listens invites truth. It honors quiet brilliance. It makes room for perspectives that don't echo the status quo.

Listening, when done with presence, doesn't just shape culture—it transforms it.

Next, we turn to leadership energy—the current beneath your culture. Because connection doesn't start with systems. It starts with presence.

CHAPTER 9

THE ENERGY BETWEEN

Engagement doesn't begin with action. It
begins with energy. ~ The BoardRoom

What if your words were the least powerful part of your leadership?

Long before your strategy is spoken, your energy is felt. Before decisions are made, it's your presence that sets the tone. And before your team takes any action, they've already responded to how you showed up.

In leadership, it's not just what you say—it's what you radiate. And what you radiate either invites alignment ... or quietly repels it.

Energy Leads First

Energy moves faster than intent. It doesn't wait for language—it reads your presence. And your team? They're already fluent in your energy.

If your presence feels scattered, rushed, or guarded, they don't need to ask if something's off—they already know. If your tone conveys doubt or control, no plan can override what's been felt. But when your presence is steady—when your energy holds space rather than pressure—trust flows. Engagement stirs. And culture exhales.

If engagement is the outcome, and listening is the path, then energy is the current that carries them both. The invitation begins with how you show up.

The In-Between Matters Most

Your culture assesses the room long before the meeting begins. Before a word is spoken, your team senses:

> *Is this room open or guarded? Are the stakes safe or unspoken? Is leadership present—or just performing?*

Culture doesn't respond to your plans; it responds to your presence—and to the energy in the in-between: the space between moments, between people, between vision and execution. This is where culture either contracts or expands. The BoardRoom emphasizes:

> The energy in between is not abstract. It's the pause between sentences. The glance that welcomes or warns. The silence that either holds safety—or fear. It's the invisible pulse that makes the visible possible.

Energetic Responsibility

As a leader, your energy isn't private—it's cultural. What you bring into the room doesn't stay with you; it becomes the atmosphere others have to navigate. This is why energetic responsibility matters. You don't need to be perfect—but you need to be aware.

Your presence is permission. It tells people whether
to shrink, speak, or rise. Before you lead the room,
your energy already has. ~ The BoardRoom

Sam's Top-Down Effect

I walked into the boardroom knowing the numbers were tough. Forecasts were off. Pressure was high. What I didn't realize—until I opened the door—was how much my energy would matter that day.

The room felt heavy. Arms were crossed. Eyes distant. Everyone was bracing for a blow. And honestly, part of me was, too.

So, I paused—not to prepare my words, but to ground my presence.

Instead of leading with urgency. I led with stillness.

I walked in with calm, not control. With openness, not performance. I observed faces instead of scanning reports. I noticed who was quiet and who seemed guarded. I let silence stretch longer than usual and filled it with steadiness, not spin.

And slowly, something shifted.

People began to breathe again. Shoulders relaxed. We didn't shy away from the hard truths—we confronted them, without flinching or pointing fingers. We moved through the tension rather than around it. We remained in it—together.

Afterward, a colleague pulled me aside and said,

"I don't know what you did, but something felt different. We felt you with us."

That moment changed how I lead.

Leadership isn't just about strategy; it's about the signals you send. And your culture? It doesn't merely react to what you say, it resonates with how it feels to be led by you.

Employees' Bottom-Up Effect

As told by Gerald

I've sat through enough executive briefings to know the drill: PowerPoint. Pressure. Pep talk.

So, when word got around that Sam was calling a team-wide meeting after a rough quarter, I figured we were in for more of the same—a scripted message, a quick Q&A, and then back to the grind.

But that's not what happened.

Sam walked in without a laptop, no slides, no assistant trailing behind him. He scanned the room, nodded a quiet hello, and pulled up a chair—right in the middle of us. Not at the front. Not at the head of the table. Among us.

> "I know the numbers are off," he said, voice steady and even. "But before we talk strategy, I just want to be here with you. Not to push. Not to spin. Just to listen—and lead from where we are."

Then he paused.

And in that silence, something settled. You could hear the hum of the HVAC, the shuffle of someone adjusting in their seat. Then, something you don't often hear in a meeting: the whole room exhaled.

No one spoke at first—but when they did, it was real. Someone admitted the pace had become unsustainable. Another said they'd been second-guessing every decision out of fear. For the first time in months, it felt like we weren't performing—we were participating.

Sam didn't rush to respond. He didn't try to fix anything or pivot to a different talking point. He just stayed in it with us—present, steady, and open.

> Later that day, I turned to a colleague and said, "It wasn't what he said. It was what he didn't carry in with him. No panic. No spin. Just presence."

That meeting didn't solve everything—but it changed something. Because when your leader shows up clear, grounded, and real, you start believing it's possible to do the same.

And that's the thing about leadership energy—it doesn't have to shout to shift the room. It just has to be honest, attuned, and embodied.

Insights from The BoardRoom

Words carry weight.
But energy moves first.

The energy between people—between leaders and teams, between ideas and action—is the invisible conductor of every cultural rhythm.

You won't find it on a spreadsheet.
But you'll feel it in the room.

You'll feel it when silence becomes spacious, not strained.
When people stop defending and start creating.
When meetings shift from transaction to transformation.

Future leaders won't just lead meetings.
They'll shift energy.

They'll pause the room before pressing forward.
They'll speak less, so others can breathe more.
They'll understand that presence is permission.

The energy you bring is the energy you build.
And your culture is reading it—moment by moment.

Energy of Alignment

You don't need louder leadership. You need cleaner energy.
Presence doesn't just exist in the room. It defines it. It's the invisible architecture of every conversation, every risk taken, and every idea shared—or silenced. It's not your words that determine what happens next. It's the energy you bring before you ever speak.
It's the felt sense that shapes what's possible within it.

In Part III, we turn to authenticity—the foundation of presence. Because trust doesn't come from polish. It comes from being real.

PART III
A IS FOR AUTHENTIC

Welcome to Part III.
This is where the performance ends. Not because polish doesn't matter—but because presence matters more.

In this section, we move beyond the surface signals of leadership and into the deeper work: alignment. That means aligning not just your strategy with your goals, but also your inner life with the outer experience of your culture.

Authentic is the third Element of the LEADER Archetype. Being authentic isn't a leadership style—it's the foundation that makes leadership trustworthy.

It's not about oversharing; it's about being transparent. It's not being perfect; it's about being genuine, especially under pressure.

In the next three chapters, we'll explore how authenticity begins with presence, is shaped by truth, and leads to trust. Without it, no message resonates, no culture connects, and no one stays engaged for long.

But when it's real—everything moves.

Let's begin.

CHAPTER 10

PRESENCE OVER PERFORMANCE

Authenticity isn't just a trait—it's a transmission.
It shapes the culture around you, whether
you mean it to or not. ~ The BoardRoom

What if the most contagious thing in your organization is *you?*

Not your strategy. Not your messaging. You. Because people don't just follow plans—they mirror presence. True presence becomes a form of permission. But what happens when your presence isn't aligned with who you really are?

In today's world of noise, skepticism, and divided opinions, authenticity isn't a luxury—it's a leadership requirement. Not for optics, but for impact. Because if your people have to wonder who you really are, they'll never fully trust where you're trying to lead them.

Realness Creates Alignment

Too often, leaders treat vulnerability like a tool—something to switch on when convenient. But your people already know. They're not just listening to your words; they're reading between the lines. The BoardRoom says:

In the future, leadership won't hinge on how polished you are—but how present you are. It won't be about who you pretend to be, but how fully you bring who you are. When you lead from the inside out, your presence becomes your power—and your culture will follow it.

Authenticity isn't optional anymore.

It's the only way leadership works now—and it will be even more critical tomorrow. Why? Because authenticity fosters safety. And safety fosters alignment. And alignment fosters everything else.

> *Performance creates a reaction. Authenticity creates a response. One is calculated. The other is connected. You don't move hearts by managing impressions—you do it by standing in your truth.* ~ The BoardRoom

Sam's Top-Down Effect

No one knew I was listening in the day I overheard a manager say, "He's probably just trying to sound relatable. You know how it is."

They weren't debating a decision. They were decoding *me*—trying to figure out what I meant beneath the message. Not what I said. What I signaled.

That moment didn't just sting; it opened something.

Because they weren't wrong. I'd been shaping my language, softening the truth, and trying to earn trust without fully offering it.

I thought I was being strategic. But really, I was being filtered. And they could feel it.

So, I stopped rehearsing. And started revealing.

I allowed people to see the uncertainty when I didn't have an answer. I voiced what I was still learning—out loud. And the change was almost immediate.

People stopped mirroring my performance and began reflecting my presence. We didn't lose strength through honesty; instead, we gained cohesion.

Because when the leader is authentic, the masks come off everywhere else too.

Employees' Bottom-Up Effect

As told by Terry

I've been with the company for almost eight years—long enough to see a dozen versions of "authentic leadership" roll through the halls.

So, when Sam started showing up in meetings a little less polished and a lot more real, I wasn't holding my breath. I figured it was just a new communication tactic—another phase that would pass. Little did I know, it was the beginning of a refreshing change.

One day during a product debrief, after a rollout that didn't go as planned, Sam looked around and said,

> "I didn't ask enough questions before we greenlit this. That's on me."

He said it like a fact. No sugarcoating. Just the truth.

Gail—who's usually quiet—spoke up next.

> "We saw some red flags on the ops side," she said, "but honestly, it didn't feel like leadership was interested in hearing it."

I waited for the backpedal—some kind of save or corporate cleanup. But Sam just nodded and said,

> "That's exactly the kind of honesty I've needed to hear. I appreciate it."

His acceptance pulled us in.

That moment wasn't just a turning point in the meeting's atmosphere—it became a catalyst for a profound change in our team dynamics.

Under Sam's authentic leadership, we gradually stopped mirroring his performance—and began reflecting his presence. And what might have once felt risky or soft turned out to be the very thing that strengthened us.

Afterward, I told a colleague,

> "It wasn't just what he said—it was what he embodied. Authenticity might sound like a buzzword, but when it walks into the room for real, you feel it.

When leaders drop the act and start showing up as themselves, culture doesn't lose strength—it finds its rhythm. It syncs. It starts to breathe again. Together.

Insights from The BoardRoom

> Authenticity isn't an image to uphold. It's an alignment to return to. It's not about oversharing—it's about not hiding what matters.

The most trusted leaders aren't the most polished. They're the most present. They don't get it right all the time—but they stay right with themselves.

They don't mold themselves into what others want. They model what it looks like to live from the inside out. Because real leaders don't ask for trust. They embody it.

Authenticity is when what you think, what you feel, what you say, and what you do all walk into the room together.

That's when presence becomes power. And that's when people believe you.

The Authentic Ripple

Authenticity doesn't stop at the top; it flows through every meeting, every relationship, and every conversation. When leaders embody their true selves, it creates a ripple effect. That ripple develops into a rhythm that others can follow.

In the next chapter, we turn to how authentic leadership influences trust, deepens relationships, and gives your culture a new kind of clarity—the kind that lasts.

CHAPTER 11

BUILT ON TRUST

Trust isn't given because of your role. It's earned because of your alignment. ~ The BoardRoom

What if the truth you're withholding is the very thing your culture most needs to hear?

If your team has to guess what you're not saying, trust is already unraveling. In moments of uncertainty, people don't need protection—they need the truth.

They need to know where they stand, what's real, and whether you'll choose honesty over optics—even when the truth is difficult. Trust isn't built in the easy moments. It's forged when leaders speak clearly through the fog.

Trust Begins with Truth

You don't have to share everything. But you *do* need to share what matters.

People don't expect perfection; they expect presence. They don't need constant reassurance; they need consistent honesty.

At some companies, leaders filter every update "to protect morale." But morale didn't improve—it evaporated.

Why? Because silence isn't neutral. It creates gaps, and people fill those gaps with doubt every time.

Trust isn't built by managing the message. It's built by modeling the truth.

Alignment Builds Belief

When your actions align with your values, trust doesn't need to be earned—it's felt. But when there's a gap between what you say and what you do, trust begins to crack.

Do you claim to value openness but shut down feedback? Do you talk about transparency but filter the truth? People don't forget the dissonance. They *live* in it.

Trust arises from alignment in action.

Action Over Appearance

You can't perform your way into trust.

Trust isn't built through motivational speeches or clever branding. It's built in how you show up—especially when no one's watching. It's in the moments when you choose clarity over comfort, substance over spin, and truth over polish. That's when people start to believe you.

When trust leads the culture, silence loses its power.
Fear stops controlling the room, and truth becomes
the most unifying force you have.
~ The BoardRoom

Sam's Top-Down Effect

I used to believe that being a good leader meant shielding people from the truth until the timing was right. When our board began discussing layoffs, I waited—hoping we'd avoid it. I kept up business-as-usual messaging, thinking clarity would come soon enough.

But clarity didn't come. And silence filled the space.

People started speculating. Productivity dropped. Anxiety grew. And by the time I finally addressed the truth, it was too late.

What broke trust wasn't the news itself. It was the fact that I hadn't brought people in sooner. I told myself I was protecting them. But really, I was protecting myself—from discomfort, from vulnerability, from admitting I didn't have all the answers.

Here's what I've learned: trust isn't built when you have certainty. It's built when you offer honesty—especially when you don't have it all figured out.

Now, I lead differently. I name what I know. I explain what I can't. I bring people in, even when the picture is incomplete.

That shift didn't make hard decisions easier—but it made our culture stronger. Because now, even in the unknown, my team trusts that I'll bring them the truth.

Employees' Bottom-Up Effect

As told by Dennis

Having worked in operations for over two decades, I've served under five different CEOs—each with their own definition of 'transparency.' More often than not, it was just a buzzword, a prelude to some major announcement that we'd only hear when it was too late to prepare.

So, when the rumors started swirling—budget cuts, consolidations, whispers of layoffs—I didn't expect much clarity. Just the usual: "Stay focused," "We're evaluating options," and "More information soon."

But one Tuesday afternoon, things changed.

Sam walked into our regular huddle holding a coffee mug, looking dead serious. She waited for the small talk to fade, then said:

> "You've probably heard the rumors. I wish I had all the answers, but I don't—not yet. What I do know is this: I won't keep you in the dark. I'll share what I can, as soon as I can, even if the picture's still incomplete."

You could've heard a paperclip drop.

Finally, someone asked, "So … should we be worried?"

Sam didn't dodge it. She looked around the room and said:

> "Yes—there's reason for concern. We're facing real budget constraints, and that could lead to restructuring. But here's what I can promise: there won't be surprises. You'll hear it from me first, not through the grapevine. And wherever I can involve you in the process, I will."

After the meeting, a colleague muttered, "Wow. No sugarcoating. That's new."

And it was.

The tone around the office changed—not because things were fixed, but because someone finally named the elephant in the room. We didn't get comfort. We got clarity. And oddly enough, that made us feel more secure.

There was a palpable sense of relief—a collective exhale—as the truth was finally spoken.

Because here's the reality: people don't break trust when they share bad news. They break it when they hide behind silence and strategy.

That day, Sam didn't show up with answers—she showed up with alignment. And from that point forward, we stopped waiting for the other shoe to drop. We started walking through it together.

The shift in our behavior was unmistakable—a testament to the power of honest communication in shaping team dynamics.

Insights from The BoardRoom

Trust is the byproduct of honest alignment.

It forms when your words, decisions, and presence all convey the same message. It evaporates the moment they don't.

When leaders speak from clarity instead of calculation, people stop reading between the lines—and start listening with their hearts.

Trust doesn't require full transparency. It requires integrity in how the truth is held.

In cultures of trust, people speak up without fear. They bring concerns forward instead of burying them. They show up to contribute—not perform.

Because in the presence of real trust, performance fades ... and people rise.

From Trust to Truth

Trust isn't something you install—it's something you reveal. It doesn't come from programs or policies. It comes from truth consistently lived and visibly led.

The next chapter explores the quiet current that underpins every culture: truth—the frequency that builds belief before anyone says, "I trust you."

Chapter 12

The Trust Channel

Truth doesn't need polish. It needs presence.
Trust isn't granted to the loudest voice, but
to the clearest one. ~ The BoardRoom.

We often discuss trust as a goal—something to build, measure, or earn. But trust isn't the destination; it's the byproduct of truth. And once trust takes root, intentional action isn't optional—it becomes the only way forward.

In today's business world, leaders are more visible than ever. Employees, customers, and partners can spot inauthenticity in seconds. Pretend alignment, forced culture, and performative leadership all fall flat.

People don't follow the leader with the best script; they follow the one who tells the truth.

Truth is magnetic. It's not about brutal honesty or full transparency. It's about energetic alignment—when what you say, feel, decide, and do are in harmony. When there's no gap between your words and your actions. The BoardRoom emphasizes:

> Truth isn't a statement—it's a signal. When what you
> say, feel, and decide are in harmony, people don't

just hear you—they align with you. That's the real work of authenticity: not to be believed, but to be felt as true. The more coherent your energy, the more contagious your culture. And that coherence begins with you.

When people believe you, they begin to believe in you. And that is the true return on investment (ROI) of leadership.

Trust Is a Two-Way Street

You don't get to demand trust; you have to give it. And when you do, people rise to meet it. But too often, leaders hold trust hostage: "Show me you're loyal, then I'll invest in you." That's not leadership—that's fear in disguise.

Real trust says: "I'll go first. I'll show up real, so you can too."

Trust grows when truth flows—both ways. Top-down and bottom-up.

When employees feel safe enough to say, "I don't know," "I'm stuck," or "This doesn't feel right," and leadership listens instead of judges, that's when cultures begin to transform.

Not because trust was taught, but because truth was lived.

People don't expect perfection—they
expect presence.
They don't need constant reassurance—they
need consistent honesty. ~ The BoardRoom

Sam's Top-Down Effect

I used to believe leadership meant shielding people from uncertainty until the picture was crystal clear. When whispers of a possible merger began, I stayed silent, telling myself I was "protecting the team."

But silence doesn't protect trust—it erodes it.

Within weeks, I could feel the shift: Meetings became cautious. Employees got quiet. People started filling in the blanks I'd left empty with their own stories—most of them worst-case.

Performance didn't plummet, but belief did.

And that's when I understood: In uncertain times, trust is your most valuable asset. Without it, every decision feels like a threat. With it, even the unknown feels navigable.

So, I changed my approach.

I called a company-wide meeting.

> "I know you've heard talk about a potential merger," I said. "I don't have all the answers—but I won't leave you in the dark. I'm here to share what I know, what I don't know, and how I'll keep you informed as this unfolds."

I didn't over-promise. I didn't spin. I simply gave them the truth I had, anchored in my commitment to keep the channel open.

The room shifted because trust had space to breathe again.

That's when I realized: Trust isn't built in certainty—it's built in the fog. And the leader who tells the truth first is the one people will follow through any storm.

Employees' Bottom-Up

As told by Zola

When the merger rumors began circulating, the atmosphere in the office shifted immediately.

Conversations turned clipped. People avoided eye contact in the hallways. Meetings felt tense and restrained.

It was clear—we were all waiting for someone in leadership to address what was happening.

But no one did.

I've been through organizational uncertainty before. I know what silence does—it leaves space for fear. And when leaders go quiet, people start writing their own narratives. Those stories? They're rarely optimistic.

What unsettled me the most wasn't the idea of a merger. It was the absence of clarity. I didn't know whether what I was hearing could be trusted.

Then came the surprise: Sam called a meeting.

He looked around, took a breath, and said:

> Let's talk about the elephant in the room. You've heard things—some of it's true, and some isn't. What I want you to know is this: you'll hear it from me first.

For the first time since the rumors started, I exhaled.

> Then he added, "I know silence creates stories. And I don't want you writing this one without me."

The way Sam said that rang of truth and sincerity.

After the meeting, I turned to my teammate Jamie and asked, "Do you think Sam's for real? I actually believe him. Do you?"

Jamie nodded. "Yeah. This is the first time a CEO has spoken directly about something important like this."

"Same," I said. And for the first time in weeks, I didn't feel like I was operating in the dark.

That moment taught me that trust doesn't require certainty—it requires honesty. And what Sam gave us that day was his word. And that's the kind of leadership that anchors a team through change.

Insights from The BoardRoom

Truth doesn't always feel safe—but it is always stabilizing.

When a leader tells the truth, they don't lose power—they anchor it. There is a quiet authority in truth that commands more than obedience—it inspires belief.

Trust is not a tactic—it's a transmission. It moves invisibly through every conversation, every decision, every silence. It begins before the words and lingers long after.

You cannot build a culture of trust without being a leader of truth.

You cannot ask people to be authentic if you have not shown them how.

If truth is the current, trust is the connection. Let it flow—through you first.

From Trust to Intentional Action

Trust doesn't end the journey—it makes the next level possible.

Once trust is established, leadership deepens from presence into precision. Because trust gives you access—but what you do with that access is what defines your impact.

In Part IV, we'll explore how to transform that trust into deliberate action. We'll move from truth to design, from alignment to intentional action. Because deliberate leadership doesn't begin with control—it begins with clarity.

And every step from here is yours to choose—and yours to lead.

PART IV
D IS FOR DELIBERATE

Welcome to Part IV.

The first three sections of this book revealed the inner infrastructure of modern leadership: presence, connection, and truth. Now we arrive at the point where leadership becomes visible in action. This is where intention meets design, where alignment turns into action, and where decisions shape not only outcomes but also culture.

Deliberate leadership does not mean overthinking. It means refusing to act out of fear, assumption, or urgency. It involves creating space—for clarity, for timing, and for what others have yet to see.

In this section, we challenge the impulse to react and replace it with something far more powerful: precision paired with presence. Once you've built trust, your team stops focusing solely on your words and starts following your energy. From here on, the decisions you make don't just shape strategy; they also signal how deeply you're truly leading.

Leadership isn't about doing more; it's about choosing what matters most—and doing it on purpose.

Let's begin.

CHAPTER 13

THE NEW DECISION MAKER

In the future, leadership won't just rely on what can
be measured.
It will be defined by what is felt, sensed, and
seen—long before the numbers
catch up. ~ The BoardRoom

Most Chief Executive Officers (CEOs) base their decisions on familiar facts and past experience. But the new decision maker, however, listens beyond what's known.

A new kind of decision-maker is emerging—one who knows that logic alone is no longer enough. In a world that moves faster than any spreadsheet can capture, the future belongs to those who lead with full-spectrum intelligence: mind, heart, intuition, and energy.

These leaders don't discard data—they elevate it. They listen to numbers *and* nuance. They rely on strategy *and* soul. They stay tuned to both facts *and* the field.

The new decision-maker leads not with certainty, but with clarity. Not with speed, but with alignment.

In an era where anyone can gather information, the edge belongs to those who integrate what others overlook: emotional dynamics, energetic shifts in a room, the silent tension between teams, the opportunity hiding behind resistance. These aren't distractions—they're signals.

Deliberate leadership means choosing not just *what* to do, but *how, when,* and *why* to do it.

And today, that depth of awareness is no longer optional. It's how innovation thrives, how inclusion expands, and how leadership evolves. The BoardRoom invites you to:

> Take off the blinders—those narrow lenses of best practices and inherited thinking. The future won't belong to those who simply repeat what's worked, but to those who listen beyond the visible. The strongest decisions are not always the fastest—they're the most attuned.
>
> When you combine data with discernment, pace with presence, and action with alignment, you become more than a decision maker. You become a movement-starter.

Energetic Authority Before You Speak

Your presence isn't just noticed—it creates momentum before you've spoken a single word. The new decision maker carries a subtle signal that others feel long before the agenda is shared.

When your leadership is rooted in calm awareness, inclusion becomes intuitive, innovation arises organically, and alignment builds—even in uncertainty.

*The future of leadership doesn't belong
to those who move the fastest.
It belongs to those who move with clarity,
alignment, and soul.* ~ The BoardRoom

Sam's Top-Down Effect

In my early years as CEO, I measured success by how quickly I moved. Swift pivots, sharp decisions, fast execution—it all felt rewarding. On the surface, results followed. But beneath it all, something was splintering: misalignment creeping in, projects lagging, and burnout building beneath the surface.

What looked like decisiveness was often an escape—from complexity, from inclusion, from the deeper insights I didn't want to face.

Everything shifted the day a crisis hit one of our international teams.

The data was clear: centralize operations, cut costs, consolidate structures. It was neat. Predictable. Logical.

Yet, something deep inside me hesitated.

I didn't make the call. Instead, I paused—and flew to the region.

I didn't stay in the conference room. I walked the factory floor, joined morning huddles, listened to the hum of machines and the rhythm of local voices. I noticed the quiet pride in people's work and frustration that their value had gone unseen.

One evening at a local gathering, I listened to their stories and sensed their purpose. I realized what we were labeling 'inefficiency' wasn't waste—it was heart. And their passion? It was a spark that simply needed oxygen.

So, I chose a different path. Instead of centralizing, I reinvested—on their terms. We redirected resources, honored local leadership, and created channels for their ideas to scale.

Twelve months later, that division outperformed every forecasted restructured model. It became one of our most profitable—and innovative—hubs.

That decision didn't come purely from intuition or solely on data. It emerged from the intersection of both. It came from integration—from wholeness—when strategy is guided by both insight and feeling, and leadership flows from both mind and heart.

From that moment on, I stopped viewing speed as a measure of success. I started asking:

"What am I missing by moving too quickly?"

And I began leading from a broader perspective—not just focused on what can be quantified, but what must be *experienced.*

Employees' Bottom-Up Effect

As told by João

I've worked in product innovation for over a decade. And I've become really good at one thing: reverse-engineering what leadership wants to hear. Pitch what matches quarterly goals. Cut out the weird ideas. Make it sound data-driven—even when your gut says otherwise.

So, when my team came up with a concept that didn't fit any strategic box—but had real heart—I hesitated.

It was a solution inspired by frontline feedback, but it lacked numbers our execs usually wanted.

Then Sam, our CEO, started asking a new question:

"What feels promising, even if we can't prove it yet?"

Amazed at the question, I decided to take a leap.

"This idea doesn't optimize current margins. It doesn't follow our usual model," I said. "But every time we show it to customers—they light up."

There was a long pause. Then Sam leaned forward.

"What do you sense here that we might be missing in the data?"

I took a breath.

"Sam, here's what we're noticing: People aren't using the product the way we designed it. They're hacking it, repurposing it, showing us what they *wish* it could do. If we tweak the design, we could unlock a whole new user segment. It's not in the projections yet—but there's energy there."

Sam didn't hesitate.

"Okay. Let's not shut something down just because we can't measure it yet. Build the prototype. Let's feel it in motion."

That prototype? It became one of our biggest successes that year.

But the bigger win was this: My team stopped playing it safe. We stopped waiting for permission. We started trusting our creative edge again.

The lesson?

Sometimes, the best decisions begin in the gut—in the messy, intuitive sense that *there's something there.*

Insights from The BoardRoom

The new decision maker's power isn't in their speed—it's in their capacity.

They hold multiple truths. They sense when timing matters. They invite voices that fear, hierarchy, or habit have silenced. They pause—not out of hesitation, but out of intention.

And in that pause, they see what others miss: the idea waiting in silence, the emotion behind the numbers, the ripple about to become a wave.

When you lead like that, you stop reacting—and start reshaping.

From Intention to Power

The new decision maker doesn't merely think—they *feel.* They don't just act—they *tune in.* When leadership merges data and intuition, speed transforms into wisdom, and decisions become invitations—not mandates.

This is the leadership edge of the future: choosing with completeness, not haste.

Now that we're leading with intention, we're ready to face an even deeper shift. It's time to slow down—not because speed is weak, but because presence is powerful.

Slowness isn't a delay—it's how clarity and courage align with timing.

In the next chapter, we'll explore how intentional slowness can become one of the most decisive and native moves a leader can make—and why the future belongs to those who know how to pause before pressing forward.

CHAPTER 14

SLOWNESS IS A POWER MOVE

Speed may deliver results, but slowness delivers resonance. The future doesn't need more movement. It needs more meaning. ~ The BoardRoom

Pacing isn't passive—it's deliberate. In stillness, leaders discover what speed never reveals.

We've all been taught that speed is essential. Good leadership moves quickly, makes fast decisions, pivots rapidly, and responds without delay. Yet, what often goes unnoticed is this: speed is not the same as momentum, nor is it the same as impact.

The obsession with speed creates more than urgency—it creates fragmentation. Hasty decisions, skipped conversations, and superficial fixes become the norm. You end up moving without progressing, acting without anchoring.

Deliberate leaders understand something different: pace shapes culture.

Slowness isn't a delay—it's a discipline. It signals that you're not driven by urgency, but guided by clarity.

Slowness doesn't mean inactivity—it means alignment. It's the pause that lets the right voice emerge, the breath that gathers collective strength, and the stillness that makes a decision complete—not just correct.

Slowing down does not mean falling behind. It means moving with completeness, allowing actions to match the depth of the moment. In today's world, this isn't a weakness—it's power. The BoardRoom urges:

> You are not here to outrun time—you are here to shape it. The pace of your leadership sets the rhythm of your culture. If you rush, others scatter. If you pause, others center. Slowness is not the absence of movement—it is the presence of meaning. It is not a lack of urgency—it's the refusal to react without resonance. The future will not be won by those who are first to act—but by those who act from fullness.

Pause with Purpose

Slowness isn't about hesitation—it's about choosing alignment over impulse.

When we pause with intention, we don't lose time; we gain clarity, uncover complexity, and protect the soul of our plans. A deliberate pause isn't a surrender to delay—it's an act of leadership maturity.

> *To lead with stillness is to lead with strength.*
> *Pause enough to notice—then act with*
> *full presence.* ~ The BoardRoom

Sam's Top-Down Effect

There was a time I believed that decisive leadership meant moving fast. Quick pivots, sharp judgments, rapid execution—it all felt like success.

On the surface, the results came. But underneath, something was splintering: misalignment crept in, projects lagged, and burnout quietly spread.

What seemed like decisiveness was often avoidance—an escape from complexity, inclusion, and the deeper intelligence that lives in silence.

Everything changed during a product launch that was already weeks behind schedule. Pressure was building, investors were calling, and everyone anticipated the usual push. But something inside me whispered, *pause*.

We pulled back—not to stall, but to listen. We held a cross-functional forum—not just another meeting, but a conversation. We extended the timeline by two weeks, which felt risky.

And in that pause, clarity emerged. We uncovered a critical tech flaw we'd overlooked. We discovered a key customer insight we'd missed. And we identified a new pivoting opportunity waiting to be seized.

Those two weeks were more than recovery time—they bought us a year's worth of brand trust and positioned us to lead, not just catch up.

Now, I tell my team:

> "We don't slow down to save time. We slow down to preserve truth."

That moment taught me that strength isn't in speed—it's in discernment. Ever since, I've built space into every critical decision—not out of fear, but out of foresight.

Employees' Bottom-Up Effect

As told by Sandy

The first time I asked to delay a launch, I braced for a flat-out *no.*

We were a week away from rolling out a major release, with plenty of executive eyes on it. But my gut was uneasy. Our user testing wasn't just mixed—it signaled confusion. Users were pausing, second-guessing steps.

So, during our project sync, I spoke up.

> "I know this is last-minute, but our testers are hesitating where they shouldn't. They're circling back and second-guessing steps. I think we're too close to see it."

There was a beat of silence. Then, our product lead jumped in.

> "We can tweak that post-launch."

But I stood my ground.

> "This isn't a bug—it's a trust break. And if we launch like this, we'll feel it in our adoption numbers."

I waited for the pushback. Instead, Sam leaned forward and said,

> "Okay. What are you sensing that we're missing?"

> "It's subtle," I said. "But users are showing us hesitation, frustration—even resignation. We've got one shot to earn their confidence. We need to listen more before we move."

Sam nodded.

"Then we slow down. Let's understand it fully before we ask the market to."

That pause changed everything.

In those extra days, we uncovered a hidden friction point. We redesigned the interaction, tested it again, and relaunched it.

The result? We didn't just meet expectations—we exceeded them.

But even more significant was the shift in how we worked.

We stopped viewing slowness as risky. Instead, we saw it as intelligence.

Afterward, I told a teammate, "I didn't know we were allowed to lead like that—with intuition, with pause, with voice."

Now, when something feels off, I speak up. Because I know I won't be dismissed. That's the power of a leader who doesn't just allow space—but honors it.

Insights from The BoardRoom

Speed satisfies the surface. Slowness reveals the soul.

When a leader slows down, they gain access to what's usually missed:

- The tension before the breakdown.

- The brilliance in the quiet voice.
- The innovation waiting for one more breath.

Pacing with intention allows decisions to form completely—not partially. You don't just choose a path; you feel its weight, its ripple, its readiness.

Slowness is how leaders shift from reactivity to resonance—from default to design.

In slowness, nothing is lost—only revealed.

From Pause to Intentional Action

Slowing down isn't retreat—it's refinement.

When leaders pause with intention, they don't lose speed—they gain substance. Hidden challenges surface, unseen opportunities arise, and genuine alignment is established—not forced.

Slowness isn't delay—it's discernment. And that becomes the heartbeat of a lasting culture.

Pausing with purpose sets the stage—but now it's time to build.

Design isn't accidental—it's a leadership choice. Built breath by breath, through conscious structure and relentless care

In the next chapter, we step beyond reactivity into leadership by choice. Because once you've created space to breathe, you must decide how to move forward—with clarity, purpose, and presence.

CHAPTER 15

LEADING BY DESIGN—NOT DEFAULT

Speed may deliver results, but
slowness delivers resonance.
The future doesn't need more movement. It
needs more meaning. ~ The BoardRoom

Much of today's leadership is reactive—constantly responding to pressures, shifting trends, and managing one crisis after another. The pace, the volume, the urgency—it becomes a cycle of surviving on momentum alone.

But leadership wasn't meant to be a reflex. It's meant to be a responsibility—and a conscious act of design.

Great leadership isn't accidental. It's a deliberate decision to lead with intention, structuring time, energy, priorities, and culture around what matters most. It's the difference between merely reacting to what's happening—and architecting what happens next.

Design isn't rigidity—it's clarity in motion.

When you lead by design, you plan with foresight. You create space for innovation. You build structures that hold firm in complexity rather than collapsing into chaos.

Design declares: *This is how we move. This is what we value. This is where we're going—and why.*

It's not just about efficiency—it's about aligning action with purpose. Not about control—it's about choosing what kind of culture you're building through every conversation, policy, and decision. The BoardRoom says:

> You were never meant to lead by default. That's the path of inherited habits, outdated systems, and unconscious repetition. When you lead by design, you become an architect of energy—not just strategy. You don't wait for culture to settle in—you shape it, moment by moment.

> Design transforms awareness into alignment, and alignment into action. It's how leaders create the conditions for others to rise.

Design Starts with Awareness

Design isn't about controlling outcomes. It's about choosing what you're willing to commit to, shape, and steward with clarity. The future won't be built by reaction—it will be shaped by leaders who pause long enough to choose not just where they're going, but how they'll get there, and who they'll become along the way.

> *Design begins in awareness. Before you*
> *structure the future, you must understand*
> *what you've been unconsciously repeating.*
> ~ The BoardRoom

Sam's Top-Down Effect

I used to think culture was something you reinforced quarterly—through programs, incentives, or strategy roll-outs. Over time, I realized it wasn't a tactic at all. Culture is shaped either by design—or by default.

Lately, ours had slipped into default.

It became undeniable: we'd hit a pivotal moment. Our leadership meetings had turned into transactional checklists. Decision-making felt disjointed. Communication was brittle at best. The results were technically acceptable—but the energy was tired, fragmented, and disconnected. Something had to change.

So, I did something I'd never done before: I paused the next 'fix-it' initiative. I gathered our executive team in a meeting—no presentation slides, no agenda bullet points, just real conversation. I simply said:

> "Let's stop reacting. Let's decide—together—how we want to lead."

What followed wasn't a workshop—it was a surrender of autopilot.

Over two days, we mapped our decision-making process and noticed what wasn't being said: tension, frustration, and unspoken assumptions. We uncovered how often we'd chosen quiet compliance over candid disagreement, and how we defaulted to our comfort zones instead of real-time accountability.

Then we rewired something more profound than process. Not a policy. Not a new task force. But our intent. We co-created decision norms. We practiced real-time feedback. We defined how we'd show up when stakes were high—aligned, present, and willing to own both clarity and uncertainty.

And the change wasn't just in what we decided—it was in who we became.

Meetings felt vibrant. Tension was acknowledged instead of avoided. Alignment started fueling energy instead of draining it. Our culture began breathing again.

We stopped leading by default and started leading by design. And in doing so, we reset everything—our energy, our engagement, and our collective capacity.

Employees' Bottom-Up Effect

As told by Colin

For years, I thought my job was to keep the wheels turning—deliver the roadmap, avoid drama, and hit deadlines. Culture? That was above my pay grade.

But over time, I started noticing the cracks. We were reacting more than leading. Priorities shifted mid-sprint. Smart people were spinning their wheels, trying to align on decisions that hadn't been clearly made. We weren't off track—we were off rhythm.

> One day, I caught Sam in the kitchen and asked, "Can I ask something kind of bold?"
>
> She smiled. "Now I'm intrigued. Go for it."
>
> "What are we actually designing? Because it's starting to feel like everyone's making guesses and calling it strategy."

Sam didn't brush it off. Instead, she nodded.

> "Yeah, I've been sensing that too. We've been moving fast—but maybe not deep enough. What would design look like from your perspective?"

That question stuck.

A week later, Sam invited a few of us to a no-slides, no-agenda session. Just one prompt:

> *How do our decisions shape the way we work—and the culture we're building?*

It got real, fast. We admitted that our decisions were reactive. Alignment was often assumed but rarely confirmed. We were choosing urgency over clarity.

> Someone finally said, "We're not broken—we've just never designed how to work together."

And the best part? Sam didn't direct from the front. She co-created with us. Together, we mapped new norms. We built intentional decision loops. We defined how we'd lead in tension, not just in moments of clarity.

After that, everything shifted. Meetings started to land better. Priorities stuck. People felt seen and included—not just informed.

For me, the shift was simple but profound: I stopped managing chaos and started designing clarity.

Because when leadership involves you in designing how the team works, it rebuilds trust and reshapes culture.

Insights from The BoardRoom

Leadership that lasts is never accidental—it's crafted with intention, alignment, and awareness.

Design is how leaders transform values into structure, vision into systems, and presence into culture. It's not about imposing control—it's about dissolving confusion.

When leaders pause to design, they create more than plans—they create conditions:

- Where truth has space to speak.
- Where alignment can breathe.
- Where others rise because the structures support—not suppress—their voice.

You weren't meant to lead by reaction. You were meant to lead by design. And when you do, your leadership stops being situational—and starts becoming scalable.

From Design to Empower

When leadership is by design, it doesn't just guide—it guides others to guide.

We pause with purpose. We re-chart our decision architecture. And in doing so, we don't merely improve outcomes; we transform the energy of leadership itself. Decisions become invitations to co-lead. Alignment becomes collective. And the results—the clarity, trust, courage—multiply across the organization.

Design sets the stage. But empowerment brings it to life. It's one thing to steer the ship with intention—it's another to release the wheel and equip others to captain alongside you.

Leadership doesn't live in the system you build—it lives in the people you empower.

As we enter Part V, Empower, the focus shifts from designing the framework to igniting the leaders inside it.

Shifting from control to courage. From structure to shared strength. From decisions made alone to owner-ship carried together.

Because design shapes the container. But empower-ment is the breath that fills it.

PART V
E IS FOR EMPOWER

Welcome to Part V.

Design establishes the structure. But culture? Culture lives in how you share it—in how power flows, how support manifests, and how people rise. Not merely because you led them, but because you equipped them to lead.

This is the moment when leadership multiplies. When trust becomes systemic. When clarity transforms into shared responsibility. When decision-making, innovation, and resilience are no longer top-down but ingrained in the culture.

In this section, we shift from designing leadership to intentionally distributing it. A culture that relies on a single leader is fragile. But a culture that empowers from the middle out? That's unshakeable.

In the upcoming chapters, we'll explore how shared power grows rather than diminishes. We'll examine how middle leaders often carry the culture more than they realize—and how the underlying systems of your strategy must align with your values.

Middle leaders are the living proof of your culture. When they are empowered, the organization no longer waits for permission—it moves with purpose.

Because leadership isn't proven by how much you carry; it's revealed by how many you lift.

Let's begin.

CHAPTER 16

POWER SHARED IS POWER MULTIPLIED

Real power isn't held. It's activated. And when it's shared, it doesn't shrink—it expands.
~ The BoardRoom

What if holding on is the very thing holding you back?

Most Chief Executive Officers (CEOs) rise to the top by proving their capability. Yet the same tight grip on decisions, direction, and control that built their influence can quietly become the thing that limits it—for themselves and those around them.

Empowerment isn't abdication. It's deliberate distribution.

It's not about stepping out of the picture. It's about shifting your role—from being the one who drives everything to becoming the one who develops everyone. This is the evolution of leadership: moving from being the center of gravity to becoming the source of lift.

Shared power doesn't dilute influence—it deepens it. It doesn't reduce accountability—it distributes it. It doesn't create chaos—it builds capability. The BoardRoom adds:

Hierarchies were never meant to be walls—they were meant to be ladders. But only when leaders stop climbing and start extending their hands do others rise.

Too many executives still equate success with control. Control over vision, decisions, pace, and perception. Yet control is a diminishing currency in modern leadership. Influence, trust, and empowerment are the new capital.

Empowerment starts at the top—but it doesn't end there. The tone you set becomes the standard everyone else follows. Your trust becomes their freedom. Your humility becomes their permission. And your presence becomes their fuel.

The strongest cultures don't idolize authority—they elevate it by spreading it.

They don't wait for a few voices to decide; they create space for many to contribute. This doesn't mean everyone does everything. It means leaders build frameworks sturdy enough to allow flexibility, autonomy, and shared ownership.

Leading by empowerment means that as CEO, you learn to discern when your presence sparks energy—and when it accidently dims the light in others.

Power held is energy contained. Power shared is culture ignited. ~ The BoardRoom

Sam's Top-Down Effect

I used to think empowerment meant delegating tasks.

I'd hand off assignments, check in occasionally, and quietly watch for signs of failure. And when they did, I'd step back in—telling myself I was protecting results.

But I wasn't protecting anything. I was broadcasting my lack of trust.

That realization hit me during a meeting when my Executive Vice President (EVP) presented an outstanding strategic plan—one I hadn't influenced. I listened attentively, didn't interrupt, and didn't try to 'improve' on anything. Her presentation resonated perfectly with the board.

Later, when I complimented her, she said words I'll never forget:

> "It's not that I needed your approval. I needed your space."

Wow! That landed like a punch and a wake-up call all at once. I suddenly realized I'd been holding my executives back.

From that moment on, I shifted.

I stopped merely granting permission and began giving power. I let go of constant oversight and leaned into co-design. I didn't just loosen my grip—I strengthened the structure that supported us all.

And I discovered something simple but profound:

When you empower someone, you're not stepping back—you're stepping forward into deeper leadership.

Employees' Bottom-Up Effect

As told by Mila

I've worked under many CEOs who claimed they wanted strong leaders around them—until you actually started leading.

So, when I joined Sam's executive team, I was cautious. I knew how to pitch 'safe' ideas and how to frame requests for 'input' when what I really needed was permission. I'd learned to manage expectations more than possibilities.

But something shifted in our culture when Sam began showing up differently.

She wasn't just listening—she was making space. She encouraged open debate, welcomed diverse perspectives, and built an environment where every voice mattered.

One day, I presented a new strategic model that was bold—and completely free of Sam's fingerprints. I braced for the usual redirect or subtle "let's tweak this" cue. But it never came. She listened, nodded, and let the strategy speak for itself.

After the meeting, I thanked her for the trust. And she said something I'll never forget:

> "It's not that I needed to approve it. I needed to get
> out of your way."

That moment flipped a switch inside me. For the first time in a long time, I felt genuinely empowered to lead without second-guessing. I wasn't just empowered—I was activated!

And what happened afterward was even more powerful: as I stepped fully into my voice, others started doing the same. Our teams became braver. Ideas grew bolder. Feedback became sharper—and more respected.

Because Sam didn't just grant freedom; she gave us the structure to hold it. She co-designed with us but never micromanaged.

> I told her later, "It wasn't the green light that mattered—it was knowing that this was *my lane to own*."

She smiled and replied,

> "That's leadership by design, Mila. I'm not here to be the smartest person in the room. I'm here to build a room full of leaders."

That's what true power-sharing looks like. When your leader trusts you with real influence, you don't just execute—you elevate. Because shared power doesn't diminish authority—it multiplies it.

Insights from The BoardRoom

Empowerment is more than a leadership gesture—it's a fundamental recalibration of how you relate to those you lead. It starts not with a memo, but with a mindset.

When a CEO chooses to empower, they're not stepping away from responsibility. They're stepping deeper into a level of leadership that trusts, supports, and activates others.

The truth is: the higher you rise in leadership, the less your success is measured by what you do—and the more it's measured by how those around you rise.

Power isn't meant to be stored. It's meant to be transferred. And in that transfer, something profound happens: performance is no longer dependent on one person (you). It becomes sustainable, scalable, and alive throughout the organization.

We've seen leaders who preach empowerment yet cling to rigid control. And we've also seen those who build systems that allow others to thrive independently. The difference is always trust.

If you want a culture of empowerment, don't just talk about it. Build it. Model it. Reward it. Create the frameworks that give it life—not just the language that makes it sound good.

Because in the end, empowered people don't just produce better results, they build stronger cultures. And stronger cultures—rooted in trust and shared power—will always outperform those built on fear, silence, or dependence.

Empowerment is how your leadership outlives you. It's the bridge between your influence today and the legacy you leave behind.

Strength in the Middle

Empowerment starts with you—but it lives in the middle.

Your mid-level leaders are the hinge of legacy. They translate your leadership, amplify your culture, and carry the true energy of your organization. When they rise, the organization rises.

When they stall, even the boldest vision loses momentum.

The middle is where alignment turns into action and where trust either deepens or breaks down.

Their choices and behaviors determine whether empowerment becomes a movement or ends at the top.

That's why shared power isn't symbolic—it's strategic.

If you want your leadership to outlive your calendar, your presence must spark theirs. Because when the middle is strong, your culture doesn't just survive—it breathes.

In the next chapter, we turn to the middle of your organization—where culture is carried, energy is modeled, and leadership either expands or evaporates.

CHAPTER 17

EMPOWERING THE MIDDLE

The middle is not where energy stalls. It's where energy spreads—if you empower it. ~ The BoardRoom

The strength of your culture is never tested at the top—it lives or dies in the middle.

So let me ask you:

> Do you know the true state of the core of your organization?

In most companies, the middle is misunderstood.

It's the place where strategy becomes execution, where vision turns into behavior, and where culture either flourishes or falters. Yet for decades, leadership development has focused on senior executives and frontline employees, leaving middle leaders to 'figure it out' on their own.

If culture is the nervous system of your organization, the middle is its spine.

Middle managers, department heads, and functional leads translate leadership intent into daily reality. They interpret your tone, carry your expectations, and turn values into action. They are the true culture carriers—and the most under-leveraged asset in your company.

Empowering them doesn't mean piling more onto their plates. It means equipping them with clarity, context, and trust. The BoardRoom reminds us:

> You can't scale leadership if you don't scale trust. And you can't scale trust if the middle is still waiting for permission.

Empowerment in the middle starts with visibility.

Visibility and Voice

Too often, middle leaders operate in the shadows—expected to execute without full understanding, lead without a real voice, and manage change without being included in the conversation. It's not intentional—it's simply habitual.

But when you involve the middle—early, clearly, and consistently—you inspire a network of influence that no top-down message could reach.

The shift is simple but powerful: stop seeing the middle as merely a buffer. Begin viewing them as bridges.

Bridges that connect teams to vision. People to purpose. Values to action.

> *Empowering the middle isn't about*
> *delegation. It's about elevation.*
> *You don't hand off responsibility—you raise it*
> *up and equip it to lead.* ~ The BoardRoom

Sam's Top-Down Effect

Early in my tenure, I overlooked those in the middle of my organization—not out of arrogance, but from a faulty assumption. I believed that if the top was aligned and the frontline was clear, everything in between would naturally fall into place.

The logic seemed sound. We had a solid strategy, a strong executive team, and clear metrics. On paper, it looked perfect.

But on the ground, momentum kept stalling. Enthusiasm was low. Execution was sluggish. Engagement scores plateaued. Despite communicating more than ever, something kept getting lost in translation.

My wake-up call came during a routine listening session. I sat across from a mid-level manager I'd never spoken to one-on-one. She looked me straight in the eye and said:

> "We're not resisting change. We're just exhausted from being the last to know and the first to implement."

That single sentence resonated more powerfully than any metric ever could.

I realized we'd been building strategy around the middle—but never with them. We'd assumed their buy-in without inviting their voice. We treated the middle like a megaphone, not a mirror.

We started changing that—slowly at first, then deliberately.

We invited mid-level leaders into strategic planning sessions—not to inform them of decisions, but to help shape them. We created growth pathways specifically for them, focused on leading culture as much as managing performance. We made space for them to question, co-create, and challenge.

But most importantly, we stopped viewing empowerment as an initiative. We started treating it as a belief.

As we did, I saw sparks reignite. These leaders didn't just rise to the occasion—they raised the standard. They built bridges between departments, clarified messages before they reached the frontlines, and became the connective tissue we'd been missing.

The results followed: faster execution, better retention, and a more unified voice across teams.

But the biggest shift?

I no longer needed to promote culture from the top because the middle was spreading it everywhere.

Employees' Bottom-Up Effect

As told by Travis

For the longest time, being a middle manager felt like being stuck in limbo.

I wasn't at the table where decisions got made—but I was the one expected to carry them out. Half the time, I heard the plan at the same moment my team did. And let me tell you—that's a brutal place to lead from.

Then Sam changed the game.

It started with a single question in a cross-functional sync. He looked at me and asked:

"What would you need to feel genuinely equipped to lead this—not just execute it?"

No one had ever asked me that. Not like that.
I paused, then said:

"Honestly? I need context. I need to understand why we're doing this before I can get people on board. And I need space to say when it won't work."

Sam nodded.

"That's fair. You deserve more than marching orders—you deserve partnership."

A few weeks later, I was invited to a strategic planning session—not as an observer, but as a contributor. I raised a concern about change fatigue, expecting to be brushed aside. Instead, I was asked to co-lead a solution team.

That changed everything.

I wasn't just executing the strategy anymore—I was helping shape it. I wasn't translating someone else's vision—I was clarifying our shared one.

Since then, our team's energy has completely shifted. There's less confusion and far more alignment. People come to me earlier with ideas—not just problems—because they know I have a voice, and I'm not afraid to use it.

And honestly? I've never been more invested.

I told Sam recently:

"I feel like I'm finally leading, not just managing."

He smiled and said, "Good. That's the point."

That's the power of empowering the middle. It's not just about creating better managers—it's about igniting a real movement.

Insights from The BoardRoom

Empowering the middle is not a management trend—it's a leadership imperative.

Middle leaders hold the emotional pulse of your culture. They know where energy is leaking, what ideas are rising, and where people are quietly disengaging. And they're often the first to see cracks long before they become fractures.

Yet they're too often placed in impossible positions—asked to lead without being led, to inspire without being inspired, to execute without clarity, and to advocate without real authority.

If you want your culture to shift, start here.

When the middle is empowered—not just informed—they unlock the energy trapped between layers. They stop translating policies and start championing purpose. They don't just cascade messages—they multiply meaning.

This is where alignment becomes action.
This is where strategy becomes culture.

This is where empowerment becomes exponential.

When you empower the middle, you empower the whole. Because culture doesn't move only top-down or bottom-up—it moves through the people who carry it every day.

A Strong Spine

When the middle is empowered, culture gains its spine—strong enough to carry weight, flexible enough to adapt, and aligned enough to transmit energy throughout the organization. This is where leadership becomes scalable. However, empowerment without infrastructure is short-lived. It requires architecture. It needs systems—thoughtfully designed, intentionally aligned, and deeply human.

The middle can only hold the culture if the systems beneath them are sound with frameworks that foster clarity, accountability, and connection. Without them, even your most inspired leaders will eventually collapse under the weight of misalignment.

The next chapter explores how to build the framework that holds empowerment in place—so the energy you've activated in your middle doesn't just ignite but endures. It multiplies. It moves your entire organization forward.

CHAPTER 18

SUPPORT SYSTEMS

*Empowerment without support is performance
without foundation.
Culture will rise—but only if the systems
can carry it.* ~ The BoardRoom

E mpowerment isn't sustainable simply because it's
energizing—it's sustainable because it's structural.

If there's nowhere for it to land, it disappears.

Leaders often talk about empowerment as if it's all
about passion and motivation. But inspiration alone
won't hold the weight of bold ideas. Without infrastructure, even the strongest intentions buckle under the
strain of inconsistency.

What good is delegation without clarity?

What value is autonomy without resources?

What promise is trust if it isn't backed by real support?

Too many cultures run on enthusiasm and
goodwill—until reality catches up. People burn out.
Progress stops. And what once felt energizing starts to
feel overwhelming.

Empowerment isn't fueled by passion alone—it's
fueled by design.

And that design must be intentional, scalable, and aligned with how your people work—not just with how your organizational chart looks. The BoardRoom emphasizes:

> Your culture is only as strong as what it runs on. If your systems don't match your values, your people will notice—and they'll adjust to what's real, not what's said.

Think of your systems—decision-making processes, communication channels, resource allocation, performance management, onboarding, even your meeting rhythms—as the silent code running your culture.

They signal what's allowed.

What's valued.

What's rewarded.

And what isn't.

When systems are built to support empowered leadership, everything changes.

People no longer hesitate—they rise. They don't question whether their authority is real or wonder if support will vanish when challenges arise. Instead of shrinking back, they step forward—with confidence, clarity, and commitment. Empowerment becomes action, not aspiration.

But when systems are intentionally designed to support empowered leadership, everything changes.

People don't wait—they initiate.

They don't ask for permission—they seek clarity.

They don't keep quiet—they lead.

True empowerment doesn't live in slogans. It lives in the systems you build, the decisions you reinforce, and the behaviors you reward.
~ The BoardRoom

Sam's Top-Down Effect

One of the biggest lessons I learned as CEO was this: Empowerment without structure is a setup—for frustration, for failure, or sometimes both.

We'd just wrapped up a major leadership development initiative. Our messaging was strong: bold thinking, innovation, ownership. Leaders felt energized. Teams were ready to run.

But within weeks, I started hearing rumblings—questions about unclear processes, clogged pipelines, and inconsistent accountability. One manager put it perfectly:

"You gave us the freedom to run—but there's no track."

That moment stung. Because I'd been so focused on inspiring change, I'd forgotten to support it. I'd built belief—but not the foundation needed to sustain it.

So, we paused and re-evaluated everything.

We mapped the systems that were quietly undermining our values:

- unclear role expectations,
- delayed budgeting cycles,
- micromanaged decision chains.

Then we rebuilt them.

We aligned workflows with our empowerment goals. We redesigned onboarding to reinforce autonomy from day one. We developed decision-rights frameworks so everyone knew who could act, when, and how. And most importantly, we trained leaders to see systems as scaffolding, not shackles.

It didn't happen overnight, but as our systems evolved, so did our results.

Engagement increased. Innovation returned. Leaders stopped asking for permission and started asking, "What else can we improve?"

That's when I knew we'd crossed a threshold:

We weren't just empowering individuals anymore.

We were empowering the culture itself to sustain and grow.

Employees' Bottom-Up Effect

As told by Anastasia

When I first heard the company's new message—"empowerment at every level"—I wanted to believe it. I'd been leading cross-functional teams for years, and I knew our people had good ideas. But we never had a path.

Then Sam made it real.

We were rolling out a new initiative, and my team had mapped a bold workflow revamp—one that would reduce wait times and cut red tape by 40%. It meant challenging some long-standing processes and trusting frontline autonomy. In the past, ideas like that died in PowerPoint decks.

But this time was different.

We presented our prototype at the monthly alignment forum. Sam didn't interrupt. She asked one simple question:

"What would it take to support this—not just approve it?"

It stopped me. Because it wasn't about defending the idea—it was about designing for it.

We dove in—discussing infrastructure, decision rights, training gaps, and budget shifts.

At one point, I admitted:

"Honestly, the idea's solid—but I'm not sure if our current systems can carry it."

Sam nodded, then said:

"Then let's change the system. Empowerment without structure is just a setup."

And she meant it.

Within a month, we'd rewritten our standard operating procedures. We created a fast-lane budget track for experimentation. We built clear check-in points—not to police, but to calibrate.

Suddenly, the system wasn't working against us—it was working *for* us.

The workflow launched. The numbers exceeded expectations. But the real win?

The very next quarter, *another team* used the same support model to push forward their own idea—without waiting for permission.

That's what happens when systems change.
I told Sam afterward:

"This time, it didn't just feel like we had a seat at the table. We had legs under the table to hold the weight."

She smiled.

"Exactly. Culture's not what we say—it's what we support."

Insights from The BoardRoom

Empowerment doesn't scale on inspiration alone. It scales through alignment—between what leaders say and what systems reinforce.

The best cultures don't just energize people—they equip them. They make sure that when someone steps forward, the ground beneath them doesn't fall away. That's what support systems are: the invisible promise that leadership won't collapse under its own ambition.

Too often, systems are designed to protect the past instead of supporting the future. Old approval flows, outdated hierarchies, and legacy reporting structures quietly erode the very leadership you're trying to build.

But when systems reflect your vision—when they align with the trust you extend and the freedom you promise—your organization moves faster, more confidently, and with greater creativity.

Empowerment becomes effortless. Not because it's easy—but because it's built into how things work.

Systems are culture in action. If you want empowerment to last, build structures that let it live and breathe.

Empowerment is the Launchpad

Empowerment isn't the finish line—it's the starting block. When leaders empower effectively, results don't just improve—they accumulate, amplify, and ascend.

Empowerment without alignment becomes noise.

Empowerment without structure becomes a leak.

Empowerment without the middle becomes a mirage.

True empowerment only becomes power when it takes root, spreads, and sustains itself.

When empowerment is no longer just a message sent but lived reality—carried by systems, culture, and leaders at every level—that's when we're ready for the real test.

In Part VI, we explore the final letter of the LEADER Archetype: R is for Result. Because the ultimate question is this: What happens when your people are truly unleashed?

PART VI
R IS FOR RESULT

Welcome to Part VI.

Every strategy leads to a result. But not every result reflects what you intended to create.

In this final section, we move beyond metrics to something deeper: the alignment between what you lead, how you lead, and what your leadership leaves behind.

Because the most powerful result of leadership is not performance—it's resonance.

It's the culture that endures. The people who rise. The values that stick. The momentum that outlasts your presence.

Results matter. But the right results—the ones that align with your vision, values, and voice—are born from within. From alignment. From empowerment. From courage.

This section invites you to see your results not just as data points, but as mirrors. It encourages you to examine what's working, what's signaling change, and what's waiting to emerge.

This isn't the end of your journey—it's the imprint you leave on others as they continue it. The future of leadership is written in the results that remain when you step back.

Let's begin.

CHAPTER 19

REDEFINING THE WIN

*Results are not proof of power—they're
reflections of alignment.
If you want better outcomes, don't chase harder.
Lead clearer.*
~ The BoardRoom

You've mastered the metrics. But are they measuring what truly matters?

In traditional leadership, results are the scoreboard. They define success. Justify strategy. Drive decisions.

But results alone don't tell the whole story.

You can hit every target—and still lose your people. You can exceed goals—and exhaust your culture. You can win the quarter—and miss the moment that really mattered.

It's not that results don't matter. It's that we've stopped asking what they mean.

What do your results say about your values? Your systems? Your leadership presence?

And most importantly—what do they say about what you're building? The BoardRoom cautions:

Performance isn't the end goal—it's a signal of alignment or distortion, sustainability or strain, life or inertia.

Reframing results isn't about being soft—it means being clear.

It means recognizing that every outcome is more than just a number. It's a cultural message. And your culture is always listening, always evaluating.

Are we achieving this because of how we lead—or despite it?

Are we growing people and profit—or one at the cost of the other?

Are we succeeding on paper—while shrinking in spirit?

These aren't rhetorical questions. They're the core metrics of sustainable leadership.

Because when the numbers rise but your people fade—that's not a result. That's a rupture.

And the cost always comes due.

True results don't merely deliver outcomes—they multiply meaning. They are byproducts of clarity, cohesion, and courageous leadership in action.

Don't let performance become a
disguise for disconnection.
Your results should echo your leadership—not
excuse it. ~ The BoardRoom

Sam's Top-Down Effect

I used to chase results like most Chief Executive Officers (CEOs) do—quarter by quarter, number by number. I equated success with spreadsheets, shareholder calls, and headlines.

But there was one year when we hit every goal—and yet something felt deeply off.

Attrition was up. Energy was down. Meetings were tense. Our customer scores stayed steady, but inside the organization, something was slipping. At first, I couldn't name it.

Until one meeting, when a senior leader I trusted sat back and quietly said:

"We're winning. But I don't think we're well."

No one disagreed.

That cut deep. I thought I was building a high-performance organization. But I realized I had built a high-pressure one!

That was the moment I knew something had to change.

It wasn't easy. I still had a board to answer to, investor expectations to meet, and a team trained to chase outcomes above all else. But I also knew this: if we kept 'winning' like this, we'd eventually fail in ways far harder to recover from.

So, I made a quiet promise—to myself first.

I stopped measuring results in isolation. I began asking what they cost—and what they meant. I invited our teams into that inquiry. I started asking them what a successful quarter felt like, not just what it looked like.

And I listened—*really* listened.

It wasn't a dramatic overnight change. We took small steps. We talked about the tension we usually avoided.

We gave leaders permission to lead with honesty, not just efficiency. And we began measuring what had long gone unmeasured.

We expanded our performance metrics to include trust, inclusion, and creativity. We tracked engagement alongside margins. We rewrote our scorecards to reflect our values—not just our velocity.

The results didn't disappear—they evolved! And for the first time in a long time, so did I—and so did we.

Employees' Bottom-Up

As told by Jack

I've led teams long enough to know how the game is played: hit the numbers, get the bonus, rinse and repeat.

So, when Sam first started talking about "alignment over output," I'll admit—I was skeptical. We were in the middle of a high-growth phase, drowning in targets. And here he was asking:

"But how does it feel to win?"

I remember thinking, *Feel? Winning is supposed to feel like ... winning.* But that quarter, it didn't.

Yes, we hit our goals—on time and under budget. But the cost was steep. My team was exhausted. Meetings were tight, fast, transactional. And honestly, I felt more like a traffic cop than a leader.

It all came to a head during an exec debrief. We were reviewing numbers, celebrating, nodding along—and then Sam looked at me and said:

"Jack, what did this win *cost* your team?"

I paused. Then I told the truth.

"Honestly? Energy. Creativity. Trust. It felt like we pushed *through* people instead of *with* them."

The room fell silent. Finally, Sam nodded and said:

"Let's not build a legacy that looks great on paper and leaves people wrecked."

From that point on, I stopped treating performance as a finish line and started seeing it as a reflection of growth. Not just *what* we accomplished—but *how* we got there.

We began tracking relational metrics: engagement scores, cross-team feedback, psychological safety. I started asking in one-on-ones, "What's fueling you right now?" instead of "What's on your plate?"

The crazy part? Results didn't dip. We got sharper. We became more agile. And when we hit our targets now, it genuinely feels like a win.

I told Sam last quarter:

"We're still driving—but now we're steering with both hands."

He smiled and said:

"Exactly. When results echo your values, they don't just prove your strategy—they prove your integrity."

That's the lesson I learned. Real results reveal whether your leadership is worth following long after the quarterly report is filed.

Insights from The BoardRoom

Reframing results is the work of an evolved leader.

It requires maturity—not to abandon metrics, but to see them in context. To recognize that numbers speak, but people echo louder. To understand that sustainable success isn't just about what you achieve, but how you achieve it—and who you become in the process.

Too many leaders are haunted by results that look good from the outside but feel hollow within. That's not leadership. That's legacy erosion.

You weren't called to deliver performance at the cost of presence. You were called to build something real. Something rooted. Something that aligns who you are, how you lead, and what your people experience.

So yes—Measure. Celebrate. Strive.

But ensure your results reflect resonance, not just reaction.

Because when they do, your impact doesn't just land. It lasts.

The Future of Metrics

The right results aren't merely earned—they're embodied. When your culture, your leadership, and your outcomes align, success stops being a chase and becomes inevitable.

If traditional metrics fall short, the question becomes urgent:

"What should we really be measuring?"

In the next chapter, we explore the new scorecard for modern leadership—one that tracks what you've done *and* who you've become. A scorecard based not only on output, but on impact. Not only performance, but resonance. Not just what you achieve—but what you activate in others.

Chapter 20

The Echo Effect

In the future, success won't be measured by what you reached—but by what you moved. Resonance is the new return. ~ The BoardRoom

Leadership leaves a trail. Not just of outcomes—but of echoes. And what echoes says more about your impact than any metric ever could.

Leaders are fluent in results—but many are starving for resonance.

Because the scoreboard tells you what happened. Resonance tells you what mattered.

Resonance is the invisible measure that reveals the deeper truth. It shows whether your leadership merely worked—or whether it genuinely resonated. It's the difference between output and impact; between attention and influence; and between presence and legacy.

Because legacy isn't built by what you say. It's built by what remains.

Traditional metrics matter—but they're not enough.

They capture reach, not depth. Delivery, not meaning. They tell you what happened—but not how it was received, interpreted, or echoed.

Resonance tells the rest of the story. The BoardRoom emphasizes:

> The most important score isn't the one you present—it's the one your people feel. Because the real measure of leadership isn't in the dashboard—it's in the undercurrent of how people experience your direction and presence every day.

True resonance happens in moments of energy, clarity, and shared momentum—long before a question is answered or any score tallied.

What numbers alone miss is the space between your intention and your impact. And it's in that space where culture is either clarified—or confused.

Ask yourself:

- Do your decisions ripple with alignment—or trigger quiet resistance?
- Do your actions invite compliance—or spark real commitment?
- Do your messages echo in values—or just repeat in words?

Because resonance doesn't just reflect performance. It reflects presence. It's not about being louder—it's about being felt.

In a world flooded with noise, the leaders who spark real change aren't the ones who shout the loudest. They're the ones who create quiet alignment, internal cohesion, and cultural coherence. They're the ones whose leadership echoes others—even when they're no longer in the room.

Resonance is your legacy in motion. It lives in the behaviors you no longer have to enforce.
~ The BoardRoom

Sam's Top-Down Effect

For years, I measured success through dashboards—financials, market share, engagement scores. If it was trackable, we tracked it. And for the most part, we grew.

But everything shifted after one unplanned conversation with a frontline employee during a site visit. I asked how they were doing. They paused and said:

> "Honestly? This place feels different lately. I can't explain it—it's like people care more. It feels like we matter again."

That comment meant more to me than any quarterly report.

It wasn't planned. It wasn't prompted. But it was true.

It reflected something we hadn't yet named—but had been striving for all along: a leadership culture that resonated.

From that day forward, I began listening not just for results, but for echoes.

I paid attention to what people repeated in their own words. I noticed the energy in meetings, not just their outcomes. I watched how decisions traveled, how values surfaced in everyday choices, how language shifted without top-down enforcement.

It wasn't always comfortable, because resonance can't be managed like metrics. It has to be felt, trusted, and sometimes led without proof.

But I realized this: resonance is the clearest signal of alignment.

It's how you know your culture isn't just working—it's alive.

Employees' Bottom-Up Effect

As told by Brooke

I've worked under plenty of leaders who could hit the numbers—but the energy always felt purely transactional. Tasks got done, but nobody's heart was in it. That changed when I started working under Sam.

She never made a show of authority. But her presence shifted the entire atmosphere. You could feel it—not in what she said, but in how people leaned in when she spoke.

I remember one team meeting where tensions were high. We were behind on a major campaign, and everyone was bracing for blame.

But instead of launching into a performance review, Sam opened with:

"What's the energy in the room right now? Be honest."

I took a deep breath and said, "I think we're tired. Not just from the work—but from not knowing if it matters."

She nodded. "Thank you for naming that. Let's realign—not just on deliverables, but on purpose."

In the weeks that followed, our work didn't just accelerate—it deepened. People stayed after meetings—not because they had to, but because they wanted to. We revisited our messaging, not to check a box, but to ensure it meant something.

The campaign ended up being our most shared one to date because it *resonated* with our audience.

Later, I told Sam, "This didn't just feel like a win. It felt like us."

She smiled and said:

"That's resonance. That's when leadership starts echoing through everyone else—not just through me."

What I've learned?

Resonance isn't a metric in a dashboard. It's how you know your culture is speaking for itself.

Insights from The BoardRoom

The leaders shaping the future are already tracking something different.

They're measuring alignment, not just milestones. They tune into energy, not just efficiency.

They evaluate decisions by how deeply they land—not just how fast they happen.

Resonance is the new return on investment (ROI).

It doesn't show up in a single report. It shows up in how people talk about the work. In how they show up for each other. In what they build when no one's watching.

This isn't soft. It's strategic.

Because resonance is what sustains performance long after pressure fades. It creates loyalty without force. It carries your message from a CEI's mouth into the culture's bones.

If you want results that last, lead in a way that resonates.

Because performance can be copied. But resonance? That's yours alone.

True Resonance

You've led. You've aligned. You've empowered. You've reframed success.

Now, as we close this section, we listen. Because the future doesn't merely respond to what we do—it echoes who we are.

And in that space—between what we said and what remains—a new kind of leadership is rising.

One that hears before it speaks.

One that feels before it acts.

One that listens not just for answers—but for alignment.

In the next chapter, we step into the quiet power that started it all—the place where intuition is honored, presence is restored, and the next era of leadership finds its rhythm.

CHAPTER 21

A FUTURE THAT LISTENS

*The future belongs to the leaders who
listen—not to control, but to understand.
Not to react, but to receive.* ~ The BoardRoom

We often ask: "What will leadership look like in the future?"

However, a better question may be: "What will it sound like?"

The future won't be led by noise. It won't be shaped by declarations, slogans, or speed alone. It will be shaped by those who listen—with clarity, courage, and no assumption.

Listening is no longer a soft skill. It's a survival skill. And more than that—it's a strategy for success.

Leaders who don't listen will be outpaced.

Cultures that don't listen will harden and calcify.

Organizations that don't listen will lose their edge, their people, and their spark.

The leaders who will thrive are those who attune. The BoardRoom signals:

Listening isn't what happens after someone speaks. It's what happens when you no longer need to. Because true listening begins when you release the need to prove, fix, guide, or react—and become still enough to receive.

Real listening isn't only external—it's also internal.

It's not just about hearing words—it's about sensing the currents beneath them.

It's energetic. It's intuitive. It's deeply strategic.

It's the CEO who walks into a meeting and feels the tension behind polite agreement. It's the executive who pauses because something doesn't feel right, even when the data says "Go." It's the leader who senses hesitation, frustration, or enthusiasm long before it's spoken.

This is the kind of leadership the next era demands—not more answers, but deeper awareness.

Because the results that truly matter won't come from saying the right things. They'll come from hearing what others couldn't—or wouldn't—yet say.

The most future-ready leaders are the ones who don't just speak vision—but hear what it's asking of them.
~ The BoardRoom

Sam's Top-Down Effect

For most of my career, I thought listening was about being polite.

I nodded, took notes, thanked people for their input. I held town halls and ran engagement surveys. I even prided myself on being accessible.

But the truth is—I wasn't listening. I was managing.

And I didn't realize it until, after one meeting, a junior employee quietly said:

"We know the talking points. But what we don't know is if anyone's really hearing us."

That line stayed with me.

I decided to change.

I stopped speaking first in meetings. I asked fewer questions with obvious answers. I became comfortable with silence. I started asking:

"What aren't we saying that we need to say?" and sitting with whatever came up.

And, then I sat with whatever surfaced. Most importantly, I began listening to myself.

Not just the polished version—but the tension in my gut when I was about to make a rushed decision. The quiet discomfort in rooms that felt off. The sense that something needed to shift—even if I couldn't explain why.

That shift changed everything.

When I listened, I slowed down. When I slowed down, I saw more. And when I saw more, I led differently.

Now I understand: Listening is not a courtesy—it's a core standard of leadership.

Employees' Bottom-Up Effect

As told by Ben

I've always been a straight shooter. I give updates, hit deadlines, and don't sugarcoat what's broken. But over the years, I learned to keep my deeper thoughts to myself—especially around senior leadership. Not because I didn't care, but because I assumed they weren't really listening.

Then I met Sam.

She didn't stride into meetings with an entourage. She came in alone, sat quietly, and *seemed to* tune into something before saying a single word.

I'll never forget one all-hands meeting where the energy felt off. People were busy but disconnected. Sam picked up on it instantly. Instead of launching into metrics, she asked:

> "What's something we're all feeling but haven't said out loud yet?"

Silence.

> Then someone muttered, "We're burning out."

> "Thank you for saying that" Sam said. "Let's stay with that for a minute."

That meeting didn't end with a to-do list. It ended with truth—and it catalyzed a profound change in how I lead.

Later, I told her, "It's the first time in years I've felt like what I *didn't* say mattered."

She smiled and said, "That's the job now. Listening beyond language. That's where leadership begins."

Since then, I've witnessed a ripple effect. Managers pausing instead of rushing. Decisions are made with sensitivity, not just speed.

It's not always neat. It's not always fast. But it's real.

And that, I've come to believe, is the mark of a future-ready culture—a culture that's adaptable, empathetic, and responsive to change. It's about attunement, understanding, and forging meaningful connections.

Because the best decisions we've made didn't come from pressure or deadlines. They came from presence—from being fully engaged and attuned to both the situation and the people involved.

That's the future I want to help build: one where leadership doesn't just fill the room—but listens to it.

Insights from The BoardRoom

A future that listens begins with a leader who listens:

- To their people.
- To their presence.
- To the unspoken truths surrounding every decision, conversation, and moment.

You cannot lead what you refuse to hear.
You cannot build cultures that breathe if you're afraid of what they'll exhale.
And you cannot create results that last if you're only focused on what's loud.

Listening is the leadership intelligence that bridges intuition with implementation.

It is how resonance forms.
It is how innovation emerges.
And it is how results become real—not just measurable.

We are shifting from a leadership era of control to an era of co-creation. And co-creation requires attunement.

Listen—not because you're uncertain. Listen because you are ready.

Ready to be led by what you hear.
Ready to be changed by what you understand.
And ready to receive the leadership that doesn't exist—yet.

The LEADER Archetype—A Threshold to the Future

You've arrived here not because you discovered new answers, but because you allowed yourself to ask better questions—the kind that don't come from the outside but rise when you finally pause long enough to listen within. As The BoardRoom says:

> The future isn't waiting for your answer. It's waiting for your attention. Lead by listening, and everything will find its way forward.

You've traveled a leadership arc few ever undertake—one that doesn't just improve how you lead but reshapes who you are when you lead.

- You've led from presence, not performance.
- You've engaged others with intention, valuing connection over control.
- You've embraced authenticity—not as branding, but as alignment.
- You've acted with deliberate timing, not just urgency.
- You've empowered others by first empowering yourself—trusting that leadership grows stronger as it multiplies.
- You've redefined results—not as output alone, but as resonance that endures.

You've awakened.

And what comes next is not just more leadership—it's the leadership that doesn't exist yet.

The kind only you can lead. Because now, you're not looking outward for what to do—you're leading forward from *who you are*.

In Part VII, we cross the threshold and go beyond the archetype.

The LEADER Archetype is your structure, your practice, and your mirror. What comes next lives beyond structure.

We now enter Stillpoint—the quiet center where leadership shifts from doing to transmitting.

Where your deepest presence meets the future before it arrives.

Where decisions rise not from noise, but from knowing.

You've done the work.

You've remembered the way.

Now, it's time to lead the future from within.

Part VII
Beyond the Archetype

Welcome to Part VII.

You've explored what it means to Lead, Engage, be Authentic, Deliberate, Empower, and create meaningful Results.

You've done the work most will never attempt.

You've peeled back the layers. Aligned. Empowered. Listened. You've redefined what it means to lead—not from pressure, but from presence.

Now, you're ready to step into what can't be fully taught—only experienced.

This section isn't about building more. It's about becoming more.

It's about the leadership that doesn't exist yet—and the one already rising within you. It's about learning to lead from a different source: not the systems you've inherited, but from the intelligence you already carry.

This is where logic and energy meet. Where outer frameworks give way to inner frequency. Where your deepest clarity becomes your most strategic edge.

Here, the intuitive leader emerges—and the future of leadership itself transcends.

Let's begin.

CHAPTER 22

THE LEADERSHIP YET TO COME

*The next era of leadership won't be defined
by who knows the most—but by who
listens the deepest.* ~ The BoardRoom

What if the future you are preparing for doesn't even have a name yet?

Most leadership models draw from the past—even the progressive ones. They're built on what's worked before. But the leaders who will shape what's next aren't merely adaptive. They're attuned.

They sense shifts before they surface.

They prepare for what can't yet be seen.

They listen beyond the noise—and lead from within.

This isn't mystical—it's masterful.

The leadership yet to come won't emerge from reinvented methods—but from remembered capacities. It will rise through the reawakening of intuition, the return to presence, and the deepening of discernment already within.

The BoardRoom emphasizes:

You don't prepare for the future by predicting it. You prepare by becoming a leader who can feel it.

Today, the world is accelerating. Complexity is expanding. Certainty is dissolving.

Yet what's needed most right now is presence and discernment—the ability to perceive what others miss.

This is the new frontier of leadership: intuitive clarity. Not the kind that replaces strategy—but the kind that completes it.

Leaders operating from this place don't just solve problems—they prevent them.

They don't just pursue growth—they guide it with intention.

They don't simply manage chaos—they hold stillness at its center.

The next frontier of leadership isn't a title,
a tactic, or a trend. It's an inner state.
Lead from that, and the world follows
differently. ~ The BoardRoom

Sam's Top-Down Effect

There was a time when I would have laughed at the idea of intuition in leadership. I believed in analytics, logic, and evidence. My calendar was packed, my decisions were fast, and I prided myself on being data-driven. If it couldn't be measured, I didn't trust it.

But over time, something began to unsettle me.

Despite our success on paper, I was losing clarity in the moment. I'd walk into meetings and feel an undercurrent of tension I couldn't name. Projects looked fine on dashboards but felt off in conversations. I was reacting faster—but understanding less. My instincts would whisper, and I'd set them aside.

Until one day, I couldn't.

We were preparing to launch a major initiative. Months of planning, airtight data—everything pointed to green. But inside, something said, *Wait.*

I couldn't explain it. It felt like pushing against a locked door.

I hesitated and brought the team together, delaying everything by a week.

That pause changed everything.

In that extra time, we uncovered a flaw with a critical vendor—a flaw that could have cost us millions and shattered client trust. Because we slowed down, we caught it. We adjusted course and launched stronger than before.

That moment cracked something open inside me.

I started paying attention to what I felt—alongside the facts I already knew. I realized my best decisions didn't come from more meetings or more data. They came from stillness, from pattern recognition I couldn't always explain, and from listening to myself.

So, I began scheduling fewer meetings and taking more walks. I started asking different questions and listening between the lines, always trusting the quiet.

In doing so, I found a clarity I didn't know I'd lost.

Today, I still analyze data and run strategy. But I also listen inwardly. Because the future we're heading into can't be navigated by speed alone. It will demand presence, perception, and leaders who can sense what others overlook.

Employees' Bottom-Up

As told by Kasey

I've worked under all kinds of leaders—brilliant strategists, charismatic speakers, and hardcore data hawks. But working with Sam? That's the first time I've worked with someone who seemed able to *sense* the future.

There was this moment during a cross-department rollout. Tight deadlines. Intense pressure. Everyone laser-focused on execution. On paper, we were fine. But the energy was off. You could feel it, even if no one said it.

In our final prep meeting, Sam leaned back, looked around, and said:

> "Something's not aligned here. Let's pause."

I'll admit—I was annoyed. We were so close to the finish line. I just wanted to push through.

Then Sam added:

> "We're not delaying because of fear. We're delaying because something unseen needs to come to light. Let's give it space."

That pause? It saved the launch.

In that space, a systems glitch surfaced—one that hadn't shown in testing but would have derailed the entire deployment. But more importantly, the pause revealed something deeper: we were all experiencing burnout.

Since then, I've watched how Sam leads. He still looks at the data. But he also tracks energy. He notices when meetings are too quiet, when "yes" sounds forced, and when tension lingers in the space between words.

I once asked him, "How do you *know* when to pause?"

He said:

> "I don't always know. But I've learned to trust when something inside me does."

That stuck with me.

I've started leading the same way. I don't bulldoze through silence anymore. I pay attention to the invisible cues—the team's mood, my own gut. And when something feels off, I check in and slow down.

That's the leadership Sam models—not through instruction, but by embodiment.

And in a world obsessed with speed, Sam reminds us that sometimes the smartest way forward is to feel what's already here.

That's the kind of leadership I practice now. And the kind I believe the future is asking for.

Insights from The BoardRoom

The leadership yet to come is already forming—in those willing to lead differently.

It's about integrating:

- Intuition as intelligence.
- Energy as information.
- Stillness as strategy.

The Chief Executive Officers (CEOs) who will shape what's next won't always be the loudest—but they will be the clearest.

They'll sit in silence longer. Act from resonance faster. And guide cultures not just through mission—but through meaning.

Because the next level of leadership isn't something you perform. It's something you become.

As the Future Arrives

The leader of the future is no longer just a role—it's a frequency. And when you align with that frequency, you become its signal. But to lead from that place, you must first learn to listen deeply to yourself. And be still enough to receive what's waiting to emerge.

In the next chapter, we'll explore Stillpoint—the inner pause where intuition is heard, presence is restored, and your next move becomes crystal clear.

CHAPTER 23

LEADING FROM STILLPOINT

*Stillness isn't the absence of action—it's the source
of it. The wisest leaders know when not to move.*
~ The BoardRoom

There is a moment before every decision. Before every
insight. Before every breakthrough.

A quiet moment—often overlooked, frequently dismissed, yet always there.

The BoardRoom and I call it Stillpoint—the sacred
pause between stimulus and response, between clarity
and action. It is not delay. It is not weakness. It's the space
that reconnects you to yourself before you guide others
to possibility.

Stillpoint is where intuitive leaders return to center.
As The BoardRoom puts it:

> Stillpoint is the place where leadership remembers
> what matters. It's where the noise drops off—and
> only truth remains.

In today's world, the pace is punishing.

CEOs are expected to respond instantly, make decisions relentlessly, and perform without pause. Yet speed does not always equate to clarity. And momentum without purpose results in misalignment.

You don't lead effectively by doing more. You lead better by knowing more deeply. And knowing begins in stillness.

Stillpoint isn't passive; it's profoundly powerful. It's where scattered energy regathers, where reactive instincts soften, and where a leader's deepest clarity rises—unforced, unfiltered, unmissable.

This isn't merely a concept—it's a capability. And CEOs who master it will not only outperform others—they'll outlast them.

> *Stillpoint is where leaders stop chasing*
> *direction and start receiving it. In that pause,*
> *alignment becomes visible, and the next step*
> *become inevitable. ~ The BoardRoom*

Sam's Top-Down Effect

I was trained not to stop; I didn't believe in slowing down.

My schedule was full. My team was busy. My mind raced with decisions. Stillness felt like a luxury I couldn't afford—until my body forced me to pay attention.

At first, the signals were subtle: persistent tension, a restlessness I couldn't explain. Then the signals grew louder—exhaustion, indecision, and the feeling that I was leading everything yet connected to nothing.

During a leadership retreat I almost canceled, I was guided through a simple exercise: sit in silence for five minutes. No agenda. No solving. Just listening.

What happened in those five minutes changed me.

I heard my own breath again. I realized how loud my thoughts had become. And beneath all the noise, I finally heard something I hadn't in months: my own voice.

In that stillness, a question surfaced—not one I expected: What are you leading toward?

I didn't have a clear answer.

That moment didn't break me. It brought me back.

Since then, I've integrated Stillpoint into my leadership routine. Not as a retreat, but as a practice. Five minutes before major decisions. Short breaks between meetings. Walks without my phone. Space for nothing—which always brings something.

Now, my team doesn't just see a busy leader. They feel a present one.

I've learned that the more I lead from Stillpoint, the less I have to force anything.

Employees' Bottom-Up Effect

As told by Adam

I used to believe that momentum was everything. If we weren't moving fast, I assumed we were falling behind. So, I kept pushing—myself, my team, the pace.

That is, until Sam changed the tempo.

It was a Monday morning leadership sync. We had a dozen pressing items on the agenda, and I was ready to dive in. But Sam opened with something unexpected:

"We're going to start with two minutes of silence."

Some of us chuckled nervously. A few looked confused. I glanced at my watch.

Sam just smiled.

> "We're not here to rush. We're here to align. Let's listen before we lead."

At first, my brain resisted. What's the point? We've got work to do. But somewhere in that pause, something shifted. My urgency softened. My focus sharpened. When we finally spoke, the conversation felt different. Slower. Smarter. More honest.

Later that week, I faced a tough decision about real-locating a major project. I began drafting my rationale and running the numbers, but something didn't sit right. Remembering Sam's words, I stepped outside for ten minutes—no phone, no checklist—just breathing and clearing my mind.

In that quiet, a better idea surfaced—an angle I hadn't seen because I'd been moving too fast. I brought it to my team, and not only did it work, it sparked an even better solution. The impact of this new approach on our team dynamics was remarkable.

Since then, I've made Stillpoint part of how I lead. It's not dramatic. It's not woo-woo. It's just effective. Now, before I lead others forward, I first meet myself in stillness.

That's where the real direction begins.

Insights from The BoardRoom

Stillpoint is not a tactic—it's a return.

A return to alignment. To energy. To wisdom that lives below the surface of urgency.

You don't need more time to lead well. You need more presence in the time you already have.

Stillpoint doesn't slow you down. It corrects your trajectory.

It lets you:

- Make the right move the first time.
- Sense what's missing before it becomes a problem.
- Feel the moment before it becomes a memory.

When CEOs adopt this way of leading, cultures shift. Meetings feel different. Decisions land deeper. And leadership stops being a chase—and becomes a choice.

Stillpoint is where vision finds voice.

It's where the next era of leadership begins—not with motion, but with meaning.

Stillpoint is not where leadership ends. It's where conscious leadership begins.

Because when you learn to pause, you don't lose momentum; you gain meaning. And when you pause long enough to feel your truth, you begin to hear what's always been guiding you.

The Signal Beneath the Noise

Stillpoint isn't a pause from leadership—it's the portal into it. When you stop rushing long enough to listen, the signal beneath the noise gets louder. And what you hear there will guide everything that follows.

In the next chapter, I'll share more about The BoardRoom—the intuitive space I trust and channel in my leadership. It's real, it's alive, and it's been the unseen guide behind everything you've read in this book.

But this isn't about accessing my BoardRoom—that's my channel—it's about discovering yours.

Because you already carry an inner voice that knows. You hold wisdom that resonates quietly yet powerfully. And you possess the intuitive intelligence the future of leadership demands.

So, you can lead from the source within.

CHAPTER 24

LEADING FROM THE INNER SIGNAL

The greatest advisor you will ever meet is
the one who already lives within you.
Listen there first. ~ The BoardRoom

The most powerful voice in your leadership isn't external—it's the internal one you've spent years learning
to ignore.

Throughout this book, I've referenced The
BoardRoom. It's not a metaphor—it's a real, channeled
space I access for guidance—a collective of wisdom I
trust and transmit through intuitive connection. It's how
I write. It's how I lead. And it's how I support the leaders
on their journey.

But this isn't about accessing *my* channel. It's about
learning to hear your own.

Because you have a signal too.

You may not call it The BoardRoom. You might not
experience it through words, images, or energy the way
I do. But somewhere within you there is a knowing. A
subtle hum of truth. A gentle pull toward what's aligned
or a pause when something is off.

That's your inner signal.

This chapter isn't to invite you into my channel—it's an invitation to discover yours.

Whether your signal arrives in silence or sensation, images or emotions, energy or stillness, what matters most is if you're attuned enough to receive it.

Because every leader has access to intuitive intelligence—it simply takes practice to tune into your signal.

Don't seek someone else's voice to lead your life. The frequency of truth was never outside you. You've always carried your own signal. ~ The BoardRoom

Sam's Top-Down Effect

For years, I didn't think I needed stillness—or even considered it.

But somewhere along the way, stillness found me.

One morning, I sat in my office staring at three memos—and realized I had no idea what I truly thought about any of them.

And that scared me more than any quarterly report ever could.

That afternoon, I did something I hadn't done in years: I closed my office door, turned everything off, and sat in silence. No plan. No agenda. Just breath and presence.

At first, it felt unbearable.

The noise in my head was still there, in fact, it got louder! Every question, every unfinished thought, every part of me trying to stay strong, right, and certain clamored to be heard.

But beneath that noise, I felt something else.

Not a voice. Not a solution. Just a quiet return to a sense of alignment I hadn't touched in years.

I sat there longer than I intended. And when I finally stood up, I knew something had shifted. Even if I couldn't name what it was.

I had made a reconnection with something still and powerful within me.

Since that day, I've called it Stillpoint and treat it as the core asset I now recognize it to be, because I understand something no spreadsheet has ever taught me: If I'm not aligned, nothing I lead will be either.

Employees' Bottom-Up Effect

As told by Jamie

I used to think intuition was just another word for "lucky guess."

My career was built on precision—numbers, trends, logic. I trusted spreadsheets far more than my instincts. The idea of gut feelings in the boardroom seemed as out of place as a yoga mat in a data center.

But then a shift occurred in Sam.

We'd just wrapped a tough Q2. On paper, everything looked fine.

But Sam gathered our leadership team and opened with something unexpected:

"Forget the reports. What's your signal saying?"

We exchanged blank looks.

I asked, "Signal?"

Sam smiled. "That part of you that knows something's off—before the metrics do. A subtle whisper, a feeling in your gut. That's your signal."

I wanted to roll my eyes. But Sam wasn't pitching a concept—he was living it.

Over the next few weeks, I watched how he led from stillness.

He'd pause mid-conversation, breathe, and say, "Let me check in with that."

One afternoon, I tried it myself. I was wrestling with a client strategy that just wasn't clicking. My brain wanted to push through. Instead, I shut my laptop, sat still, and asked, "What's not aligned here?"

A quiet phrase surfaced in my mind: *You're solving the wrong problem.*

I opened the brief, reread it, and suddenly saw it. We'd been framing the wrong outcome. I adjusted one core question—and everything fell into place.

Now, I've made it a habit. A quiet moment before big decisions. A breath before I speak. A check-in before I charge ahead.

Sam didn't just model a better way to lead. He modeled a deeper way of listening—one that starts from within.

Insights from The BoardRoom

Your inner signal is not a mystical fluff—it's the core of your leadership.

It's the place where logic and intuition collaborate.
Where strategy and soul integrate.
Where presence becomes power.

Too often, CEOs rely on everything but themselves: market reports, opinion polls, and consultant roadmaps.

All of that has value. But none of it replaces the quiet, wise voice within you—the one that always tells the truth, even when it's inconvenient.

In the future of leadership, developing a relationship with your signal won't be optional. It will be essential.

Because once you know how to sit with it, listen to it, and move from it:

- You stop chasing external validation.
- You lead from trust.
- You move in integrity.
- You make decisions that resonate.

And your team, your culture, and your legacy?

They feel the difference.

Because when you're aligned with your signal, your leadership starts transmitting clarity.

From Knowing to Leading

Your inner signal isn't a whisper to ignore—it's a frequency to follow. When you lead from that deep inner knowing, you stop performing and start transmitting. Alignment becomes action. Leadership becomes resonance.

One chapter remains—the threshold between knowing and becoming.

You've awakened the intuitive leader within. You've learned to listen beneath the noise, to pause under pressure, and to trust the quiet signal within that guides you.

Now comes the true test: to lead from that place. Boldly. Unapologetically. Without turning back.

CHAPTER 25

BE THE DIFFERENCE—NOW

*There comes a moment in every legacy where
the question is no longer what have you built, but
what have you awakened?* ~ The BoardRoom

You've led.
    You've delivered.
You've endured.

You've carried the weight of decision, direction, and consequence. And now—at this very moment—you stand at a different kind of edge.

Not the edge of another fiscal year.

Not the edge of a strategic plan.

But the edge of leadership itself.

Standing at the Edge of Now

What if this is the moment—the one where everything you've learned, questioned, and withheld finally converges?

Not to recreate what you've always known—but to lead what doesn't yet exist.

Because the future of leadership isn't waiting for more credentials.

It's waiting for someone willing to *become* the example.

To live it before it's proven.

To lead it before it's accepted.

You are that someone.

Where Personal Awakening Meets Cultural Activation

This book was never here to hand you answers. It came to remind you of the truth you've always carried. The part of you that recognizes truth the moment it resonates and is exhausted by performance, pretending, and polish.

You've remembered:

- Leadership isn't performance—it's presence.
- Culture isn't commanded—it's embodied.
- Trust isn't forced—it flows from alignment.

But this isn't just about *you.*

It's about what you activate in others—starting now. Because awakened leadership doesn't scale through training. It scales through alignment.

Training teaches leaders what to do. Alignment reminds them who they are.

As The BoardRoom reminds us:

> You cannot package presence, clarity, or intuitive knowing into a slide deck.
> You awaken leadership not by imposing systems—but by unlocking truth.

So, ask yourself these two questions:

1. Will you keep managing outcomes?
2. Or will you start moving culture?

The Leadership Waiting to Be Born

Right now, your people are watching.

Right now, someone is deciding whether to speak their truth.

Right now, a future leader is waiting for a signal—your signal.

You cannot scale what you do not live.

You cannot teach what you do not embody.

The BoardRoom emphasizes:

> Cultural coherence begins within—when leaders align with themselves, with one another, and with the purpose they serve.

When alignment takes root, awakened leadership grows exponentially. It becomes magnetic. Contagious. Alive.

You must become the leadership you wish to grow. And grow it with clarity, energy, and relentless intention.

This is how cultures breathe.

This is how trust builds.

This is how the future forms—through you.

Your Call to Be the Difference

This chapter doesn't close the book. It opens the next door to everything that follows.

Your legacy won't be measured by the metrics you managed. It will be remembered by the courage you modeled—and amplified through the alignment you inspired.

Be the tone.

Be the shift.

Be the one who chooses truth over ease.

Because the moment a leader breathes from truth, culture exhales.

Truth steadies the leader.

Culture feels it—and relaxes.

The future feels it—and responds.

As The BoardRoom says: "One honest breath allows everything to align."

That breath is just the beginning.

To lead what's next, truth must go deeper—

Not just felt but lived.

Not just spoken but shared.

This is where alignment becomes leadership.

The leaders of tomorrow won't be defined by
what they know—but by how fully they align.
Presence will replace posturing. And
those who lead from truth
will carry the future in every decision they make.
~ The BoardRoom

Sam's Top-Down Effect

There came a point when I realized—the world I was leading wasn't the one I'd been trained for.

The playbooks no longer fit.

The metrics felt flat.

The leadership I had mastered wasn't resonating.

My instincts were telling me something the systems couldn't:

What got you here won't take us forward.

At first, I resisted. I doubled down—more structure, more certainty, more control.

But it only widened the gap between who I was … and who I was becoming.

Everything shifted when I stopped asking, "What's the right answer?"

And started asking, "What feels aligned?"

I stopped trying to be impressive. And started trying to be present.

I brought stillness into decisions. I let intuition sit at the table.

I trusted what I felt—not just what I could prove.

It wasn't about abandoning logic. It was about integrating something deeper.

Slowly, everything changed.

Meetings felt real. The culture softened—and strengthened.

People spoke more honestly and moved more purposefully.

Because I wasn't just leading a team. I was modeling a new way to lead.

I used to think leadership was about getting it right. Now I know—it's about being real enough that others rise with you.

I'm not just building the business anymore.

I'm becoming the signal that sets it free.

Employees' Bottom-Up Effect

As told by Conrad

I'll never forget the day Sam pulled me aside.

We were prepping for a high-stakes launch. Deadlines. Chaos. Pressure from every angle. And I was holding it all—tight.

> Sam asked, "Do you feel like you're leading—or just holding it together?"

> "Honestly?" I said, "Most days, it feels like survival."

She nodded.

> "You don't have to lead like the version of you that got promoted. You can lead from the version that's evolving."

That cracked something open.

I stopped pretending I had all the answers.

I started showing up with more honesty.

I began leading from alignment—not just obligation.

I used to think culture came from the top. Now I know—it's carried by the middle.

By people like me.

Leaders in the trenches.

Modeling the shift every single day.

Every pause.

Every truth spoken.

Every moment we lead from who we are—it adds up.

Sam didn't just lead differently. She gave us permission to evolve.

> Now when I walk into a room, I don't ask, "What needs to get done?" I ask, "What's ready to rise?"

Because I've learned something powerful:

> You don't have to wait to be the difference. You can be it now.

Insights from The BoardRoom

You've been searching for a new model of leadership. But it's already in you.

It's not a framework.

Not a formula.

It's a frequency.

The signal of a leader who has stopped outsourcing their power.

The presence of a leader who no longer needs to be validated to be trusted.

The clarity of a leader who listens—before they act.

You don't need more time.

You need more truth.

When you lead from alignment, you don't chase outcomes.
You generate resonance.

The world doesn't need more control.
It needs more coherence.

And those who will shape what comes next?
They'll be the ones bold enough to be coherent with themselves first.

That's who you are now.

Don't wait.
Don't shrink.
Don't go back.

You've remembered what leadership can be.
Now go build it.

The Next Chapter Is Yours

You've reached the end of this book—but the true beginning lies ahead.

You've awakened.

You've remembered who you are beneath the title.

You've reclaimed the way leadership feels when it's led from within.

Now it's time to build what can hold that awakening. Because the cultures we need next must reflect not who we've been—but who we're becoming.

We're bringing breath, energy, and human intelligence into the systems that shape our work and lives. We're redesigning how we lead, how we connect, how we trust, and how we grow—together.

So, take a breath.

Then step forward.

You've remembered the signal.

Now build the culture bold enough to carry it.

COMING SOON!

Be The Difference Now:
The Culture We Build Next

What happens after a leader evolves?

They build something bigger.

As the second book in the four-part *Be The Difference Now* series, *The Culture We Build Next* shifts the focus from personal leadership to collective impact. Donna shows you how to create cultures where truth builds trust, power flows instead of clings, and every voice carries weight.

This is more than a follow-up—it's an activation. You'll explore how to design, nurture, and sustain workplaces where presence, purpose, and participation are the norm—not the exception. It's a call to all CEOs, team leads, and culture carriers ready to breathe life into organizations they've been waiting for—places where values aren't slogans, but the way work feels.

Drawing from real-world stories and emerging organizational models, Donna invites you to co-create the workplaces we all long for—where trust runs deep, power is shared, and every voice matters.

The journey doesn't end here.

Book 3 – *Lead the Culture or Lose It* delivers the CEO blueprint for protecting and amplifying the culture you've built. **Book 4 – *The Culture We Breathe Forward*** takes us even further, revealing how to design organizations that remember who they are and carry their values forward for generations.

Whether you're a CEO, a team lead, or a culture carrier in your corner of the company, this book is your guide to being the difference—not just in how you lead, but in the world you help shape.

If the first book awakened your leadership, *The Culture We Build Next will awaken your world.*

Be the first to know when it's released at www.BeTheDifference.global.

TEASER

The Culture We Build Next

The air in your company tells the truth—long before any-one speaks.

Your numbers look solid. Your team looks steady. Your brand story sparkles on the slides.

But if you're honest, you feel it:

A tightening.

A hush.

A subtle stiffness in the room.

A silence that whispers:

We're performing …

not breathing.

The culture you're leading today was built for the leader you used to be.

It carried you here. But it will not carry you forward.

Because culture isn't policies or posters or clever phrases in the lobby.

Culture is air.
It's the frequency people feel the moment
you enter the room. ~ The BoardRoom

When your leadership evolves—but your culture doesn't—you'll feel it:

- Meetings fall silent.
- Energy shrinks.
- Conversations tiptoe around truth.
- Your presence feels heavier than it should.

That's not dysfunction.

That's contraction.

It's your system telling you:

This atmosphere no longer fits who you've become.

Most leaders try to fix this with new programs, new slogans, new incentives.

It doesn't work.

Because culture doesn't shift through language.

It shifts through breath.

Through presence.

Through the energy you transmit in every conversation, decision, and silence.

The real question isn't:

Is your culture working?

The real question is:

Is your culture awake?

In this next book, we won't patch the old—we'll build the new.

A culture that breaths with you and pulses with trust and truth.

Because the next era of leadership isn't built on structure, it's built on the energy that moves through it.

Are you ready?

Not to fix ...

to design.

Let's design the culture you—and your people—can finally breathe in.

Right now, the future is calling for leaders brave enough to expand the air around them instead of compressing it.

You are that energy. ~ The BoardRoom

AFTERWORD

Writing *Be The Difference Now* has been a journey of reflection and awakening.

In these pages, I've shared lessons drawn from decades in executive leadership, but more importantly, I've shared the inner work that transformed the way I lead—and live. This journey reinforced a truth I've long believed: leadership is alive, never static. It shifts and expands in step with our own evolution. And when we change, everything we touch is invited to change with us.

Through The BoardRoom, I've learned that the greatest shift in leadership isn't in what we do, but in how we *be*. It's the unseen energy—presence, alignment, and resonance—that shapes the cultures we nurture and futures we create.

My ask of you is this:

> Do not wait for permission to lead differently. Step fully into your own alignment, trust your inner knowing, and become the presence your world has been waiting for. Be the difference now—because the future depends on it.

I am deeply grateful to the mentors, colleagues, and friends who have walked this path with me, and to the leaders who have trusted me to join their journey.

And to you, the reader—thank you for bringing your time, attention, and heart into these pages. In choosing to read this book, you've already joined the movement to lead in a different way.

This is only the beginning.

My next book, *The Culture We Build Next*, expands the conversation from personal leadership to the collective cultures that pulse with truth, trust, and energy. *Be The Difference Now* was about awakening the leader within; my next book is about breathing life into the world you lead.

The work of leadership will never be finished—but it will always be worth it.

Lead with presence. Lead with truth. Lead with resonance.

Lead this way—and watch the world rise to meet you.

You are the difference.

Warm regards,
Donna

Be The Difference Now

RESOURCES TO LEAD WHAT'S NEXT

Leadership shifts when you do—from pressure to presence, from tactics to truth.

Step into a curated library for leaders who build what doesn't yet exist. Here you'll find my most potent tools in one place: timeless frameworks, activation decks, executive insights, Stillpoint practices, transformational journeys, and advisory programs for CEOs and teams.

Whether you need a five-minute reset or a full cultural realignment, these resources meet you at the edge of growth and move you forward with clarity, cohesion, and steady power. *The BoardRoom* invites you to start where you are, go as deep as you're ready, and return to the work with a renewed signal and confident presence.

Explore everything at www.BeTheDifference.global

The Twelve Laws of Leadership (Free PDF)

Leadership that lasts isn't powered by quick tactics—it's grounded in timeless truth.

These twelve laws form the energetic foundation of the LEADER Archetype, showing you how to lead with integrity, clarity, and resonance—especially when conventional strategies no longer work. More than principles, they serve as both a diagnostic and a roadmap for navigating leadership in a new era.

Download at www.BeTheDifference.global/free

The LEADER Activation Deck

Your pocket-sized catalyst for conscious leadership.

Designed as the perfect companion to *Be The Difference Now*, this deck works solo or with a team in meetings, retreats, or workshops. Pull a card, reflect on its message, and turn to the matching section of the book for deeper insight.

Get the deck at www.BeTheDifference.global/deck

Executive Insights Portal

A private hub for visionary leaders ready to elevate presence and impact. Inside you'll find two transformative resources:

- **Executive Insights Blog and Articles**—Monthly transmissions from *The BoardRoom* blending intuitive guidance, cultural-alignment strategies, and actionable leadership insights to sharpen decisions, amplify influence, and spark culture-wide shifts.
- **Executive Codes and Activations**—Frequency-based tools that recalibrate energy and reset leadership in real time. Each of the codes offers a targeted energetic upgrade; each activation anchors the shift, so it shows up in your culture immediately.

Access at www.BeTheDifference.global/executiveinsights

Private Channeling Session with *The BoardRoom*

When clarity can't wait, truth leads.

Bring your most urgent questions, pivotal decisions, or cultural challenges into a private session with *The BoardRoom*. These aren't ordinary conversations—they're intuitive transmissions that cut through noise, reveal next steps, and align you with the future you're meant to create.

Book at www.BeTheDifference.global/boardroom

Stillpoint Portal

Your gateway to practices and experiences that return you to clarity, presence, and decisive action. Begin with quick resets or dive into deeper immersions—each designed to quiet the noise and realign your leadership from the inside out.

- **Stillpoint Activations (Free)**—Guided audio resets for real-time clarity and energetic alignment.
- **Stillpoint Alignment Sessions**—From a single hour to a two-day immersion, these sessions recalibrate your energy, recenter your presence, and realign leadership to what's true.

  - **Clarity at Your Core (1-Hour Immersion)**—A private reset for CEOs and executives focused on presence over performance.

- **One-on-One Breakthrough**—A focused hour to clear interference and reconnect to the inner signal that drives aligned action.
- **Stillpoint for Teams (2-Day Immersion)**—Rebuild cohesion, realign vision, and reset leadership tone at the top.

Enter at www.BeTheDifference.global/stillpoint

Transformational Experiences: Accessing the Wisdom Beneath Leadership

True leadership doesn't start in the mind—it begins deeper, in the patterns, stories, and energetic signals that quietly shape how you lead. These guided experiences bypass surface thinking to dissolve what no longer serves and activate the presence your culture is waiting for.

Available Experiences: Hypnosis for Leaders; Past Life Regression; Future Life Progression; Life Between Lives.

Explore at www.BeTheDifference.global/experiences

The CEO Alignment Suite Programs

Because some transformations require both a container and a catalyst.

For CEOs ready to lead from alignment rather than exhaustion, these programs provide strategic recalibration and immersive clarity to help you return to truth before taking your next step.

1. **Individual Alignment**—Focused one-on-one support.

   - Executive Advisory Partnership
   - Breakthrough Intensives
   - Clarity at Your Core (A 60-minute virtual Stillpoint)

2. **Team and Culture Immersions**—Unify leadership teams and accelerate cultural alignment.

   - Unified: The Executive Team Realignment (two-day immersion)
   - Vision and Culture Alignment Intensive
   - CEO Convergence Circle (48-hour gathering)

3. **Advanced Pathways**—Expand your influence and certify new ways of leading.

   - LEADER Archetype Certification (8 Weeks)
   - Custom Executive Immersions

Learn more at www.BeTheDifference.global

CEO Consulting with Donna DiDomenico
For visionary CEOs and executive teams ready to stop running on pressure and start leading from presence, I offer focused, high-impact consulting that cuts through noise and delivers strategic clarity. Whether you need a private breakthrough session or a full-team recalibration, these advisory experiences bring practical insight and energetic alignment to every decision.

Schedule at www.BeTheDifference.global/consulting

About Donna

The leaders of the future won't rise by repeating the past. They will rise by expanding who they are and by shaping cultures that breathe with them.

Donna DiDomenico is a catalyst for this evolution.

With more than four decades of executive leadership at Amtrak, the New Jersey Legislature, New Jersey State Police, The Vitamin Shoppe, and W.W. Grainger, Donna understands the weight—and the cost—of high-stakes decision-making.

But it is her energetic intelligence—her ability to sense alignment, expand contraction, and nurture that sets her apart as a trusted guide for CEOs ready to transform and lead at a deeper level.

Her own awakening came in Washington, D.C., through a near-death experience that redefined her purpose and unlocked a profound connection to the unseen dimensions of leadership.

Now, through her partnership with The BoardRoom, Donna channels the collective wisdom of leaders who operate beyond the visible edge of business.

She helps senior executives feel the truth of their leadership, awaken the pulse of their culture, and activate a presence that speaks to people before words ever do.

Donna is the founder of BeTheDifference.global, author of *Be The Difference Now* and co-author of

The Power and Impact of Courageous Changemakers and creator of the LEADER Archetype—a model that fuses strategy with soul, data with discernment, and logic with intuitive intelligence.

Her work equips senior leaders to see what others miss, trust what they feel, and design cultures rooted not in control—but in resonance, truth, and transformation.

For CEOs willing to step into the next era of leadership, Donna doesn't just teach transformation—she *transmits* it.

Her presence leaves an impression felt long before it's fully understood.

When I'm Not Working with CEOs

When I'm not guiding executives to become the leaders of tomorrow, I'm home in Hamilton, New Jersey, sharing everyday adventures with my husband Anthony, delighting in heart-to-heart moments with our daughter Alyssa, and soaking up the love of our two playful pups, Bella and Cooper.

www.ingramcontent.com/pod-product-compliance
Lightning Source LLC
Chambersburg PA
CBHW071644200326
41519CB00012BA/2392